Victorian Gingerbread

Patterns & Techniques

Patrick Spielman
& James Reidle

Sterling Publishing Co., Inc.   New York

Library of Congress Cataloging-in-Publication Data

Spielman, Patrick E.
    Victorian Gingerbread : patterns & techniques / Patrick Spielman &
James Reidle.
        p.   cm.
    Includes bibliographical references and index.
    ISBN 0-8069-7452-4
    1. Fretwork.   2. Jig saws.   3. Decoration and ornament—Victorian
style.   I. Reidle, James.   II. Title.
    TT186.S677   1992
    745.51—dc20   92-19160
                                                                          CIP

Published in 1992 by Sterling Publishing Company, Inc.
387 Park Avenue South, New York, N.Y. 10016
© 1992 by Patrick Spielman and James Reidle
Distributed in Canada by Sterling Publishing
% Canadian Manda Group, P.O. Box 920, Station U
Toronto, Ontario, Canada M8Z 5P9
Distributed in Great Britain and Europe by Cassell PLC
Villiers House, 41/47 Strand, London WC2N 5JE, England
Distributed in Australia by Capricorn Link Ltd.
P.O. Box 665, Lane Cove, NSW 2066
Manufactured in the United States of America
All rights reserved

Sterling ISBN 0-8069-7452-4

1   3   5   7   9   10   8   6   4   2

CONTENTS

Acknowledgements 4

Introduction 5

1 Basic Materials 11

2 Basic Layout Techniques 16

3 Tool Processes 21

4 Flat, Sawn Brackets 30

5 Corbels 77

6 Shelves 91

7 Fan Brackets 94

8 Grilles and Spandrels 104

9 Porch Spandrels 108

10 Sawn Balusters 116

11 Running Trim 122

12 Headers 127

13 Valances 138

14 Gable Ornaments 147

15 Screen Doors 158

16 Picket Fences and Trellises 161

17 Victorian Mailboxes 165

18 Victorian Signs 176

19 Finishing and Installation 187

Metric Equivalents 190

About the Authors 191

Index 192

Color Section Opposite Page 64

ACKNOWLEDGMENTS

We extend our sincere appreciation and thanks to Dirk Boelman of the Art Factory and to his assistant, Sharon Raines, for producing all the line art in this book. We also express our special gratitude to Grant Lanceleve of Sydney, Nova Scotia; to Honeytree Wood Shop of Red Oak, Texas; and to Silverton Victorian Millworks of Durango, Colorado, for providing excellent illustrations showing some of their work and products. Thanks to Carl Weckhorst for helpful photos and to Sherri Valitchka for her computer work. Thanks to our excellent typist, Julie Kiehnau, for her efforts.

We also thank and appreciate those who took a keen interest in our work and lent their support in a variety of ways. Special thanks to Pierre Gilson of the Radford Millwork Co. of Oshkosh, Wisconsin, for providing reference materials and assistance in our research of old designs and patterns—many of which are reproduced here.

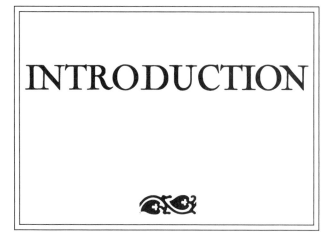

INTRODUCTION

This book is an accumulation of many old designs and ornamental patterns typical of those that decorated homes and commercial buildings during the Victorian era (approx. 1830–1910). See Illus. i.-1. Many terms are used to describe this form of architectural ornamentation. The most common is "Victorian gingerbread," named for the sugar frostings common on German gingerbread houses. However, this form of fancy architectural trimmings has also been called carpenter's lace, bric-a-brac, carpenter Gothic, and architectural fretwork.

In recent years there has been a healthy movement across the United States and Canada to preserve and reconstruct elegant Victorian buildings that have beautiful ornamental woodwork both inside and out. It is becoming increasingly popular to build new homes and commercial buildings featuring Victorian gingerbread (Illus. i. 2–5). According to *Victorian Accents* magazine, "entire new-Victorian developments are now springing up in the mid-West, California, and in the Northeast."

Also noticeable in many areas are contemporary homes fitted with copies of Victorian gingerbread ornamentation. The addition of gable decorations (Illus. i. 3–5) or a pair of sawn brackets installed at squared openings visually suggests a transformation from contemporary to Victorian.

The use of Victorian gingerbread makes a definite design statement. It shows a vivid appreciation for those craftsmen and woodworking artists whose works varied from very simple to the very ornate. Unsurprisingly, the most ornate and finely crafted gingerbread was found on mansions owned by wealthy industrialists and merchants.

INTERIOR ARCH GRILLE COLONNADE

COLONNADE ARCH GRILLE No. 4384

DESCRIPTION

Top grille drop to cap 18 inches.   Height of pedestals 30 inches.   Width of pedestals made in proportion to size opening ordered.   Columns are 5 inches in diameter tapering to $3\frac{1}{2}$ inches at neck.

PRICES

Any height not exceeding 9 feet

Width of opening not to exceed   6 feet $47.60
Width of opening not to exceed   7 feet 49.00
Width of opening not to exceed   8 feet 50.40
Width of opening not to exceed   9 feet 51.80
Width of opening not to exceed 10 feet 53.20

Above prices cover work made of Oak, Yellow Pine, Birch, Cypress or woods of equal value, in the white, ready for finishing.

Illus. i-1. Interior design of an authentic Victorian grilled arch. The lower ceilings in modern homes would not allow room for this today. However, similar grilles are now used commercially in restaurants and hotels. This illustration is reproduced from the early Victorian Millwork Product Catalog of Segelke & Kohlhaus Mfg. Co., of La Crosse, Wisconsin. Note the prices.

Illus. i-2. Modern Victorian ornamentation of interior openings. Note the grooved casings and corner-block construction with simple butt-joint corners as opposed to conventional mitres. (Design and fabrication by Honeytree Wood Shop).

Illus. i-3. Victorian gable decoration on a modern brick ranch-style home. (Photo courtesy of Honeytree Wood Shop.)

Illus. i-4. Simple sawn brackets and gable ornamentation give a Victorian effect to this conventional two-story home. (Photo courtesy of Grant Lanceleve.)

Illus. i-5. Close-up of a sawn bracket installed on a garage-door corner. (Photo courtesy of Grant Lanceleve.)

Less elaborate gingerbread was found on smaller homes and in rural areas. Most gingerbread was used for ornamentation and visual embellishment rather than for structural support.

Today, many mail-order companies specialize in the manufacture of Victorian millwork and gingerbread components. Building supply centers now carry some of the more common millwork selections of brackets, turnings, and mouldings.

Victorian gingerbread is now very easy for the do-it-yourselfer to make. The growing interest in new Victorian construction, along with the ongoing interest in refurbishing or restoring old, authentic Victorian homes, offers very lucrative opportunities for enterprising woodworkers and requires few special tools. The new, constant-tension scroll saws and narrow scrolling blades available for home-shop band saws make it easy to construct almost any imaginable Victorian design in thick woods. Thinner and less sharply curved ornaments can be cut easily with coping saws, hand-held portable scroll saws or sabre saws.

This book provides copies of many authentic Victorian gingerbread designs. We have generally reduced the originals to half size, which we consider more appropriate for contemporary building trends. Occasionally, patterns are presented in their original Victorian size. Of course, any pattern may be altered to accommodate your individual requirements.

Many of the designs for brackets, corbels, headers, gable brackets and running trim in this book were copied from turn-of-the-century catalogs. Others are one-of-a-kind creations copied from pieces found in old homes and buildings. Some of the early millwork-company catalogs from which the designs in this book were adapted and copied include the Foster-Munger Co., of Chicago; the Radford Bros. and Co., of Oshkosh (Wisconsin) and Chicago; the Segelke & Kohlhaus Mfg. Co., of La Crosse, Wisconsin; the Redford & Wright Co., of Duluth, Minnesota; the Adams & Kelly Co., of Omaha; and the Gould Mfg. Co., of Oshkosh.

It should be noted here that the Wholesale Sash, Door, and Blind Mfg. Association published a book of over 400 pages at the turn of the century entitled *The Universal Design Book*. It contained numerous illustrations of products identical to those presented in individual manufacturers' product catalogs. Consequently, it is often difficult to establish where any individual design actually originated.

This book is arranged by subject. It includes the selection of materials, and covers basic techniques for layout, cutting, assembly, finishing and installation. You will also find numerous tips and information about easy-to-make jigs, which should make your working hours easier, more accurate, and more fun.

You will quickly see how easy and affordable making your own Victorian gingerbread can be. Once you realize the visual impact of gingerbread on interior and exterior home decoration, you will find many places to use it. Indoors, you can span gingerbread over the kitchen and bathroom sink or tub areas and extend ornamentation between cabinets (Illus. i.-6). Create elaborate room dividers, decorate openings between rooms, finish wall shelves, mantels, and the like easily with brackets or custom spandrels to create a truly Victorian atmosphere quickly and easily.

Illus. i-6. Combining basic Victorian gingerbread components creates this custom decoration very easily. Here, narrow ball-and-dowel spandrels coupled with two fan brackets are adapted to a specific opening. (Photo courtesy Honeytree Wood Shop.)

Illus. i-7. Gingerbread ornamentation on this two-story home totally transforms its character. (Photo courtesy of Grant Lanceleve.)

Delightful gingerbread ornamentation can be applied in one form or another to almost any existing building and to whatever degree you may desire. See Illus. i.-7.

Finally, to tie all the design elements together, we have included complementary designs for fencing, mailboxes (Illus. i.-8), house numbers and signs — right down to a handsome welcome sign designed with true Victorian elegance.

Illus. i-8. A rural mailbox with a Victorian motif. See page 173 for details.

BASIC MATERIALS

The most inexpensive way to decorate with Victorian gingerbread is to purchase the wood and make most of the gingerbread yourself. Buy ready-made just those extras that you can not or do not want to make yourself. It is probably more cost effective to buy dowels, round balls, and turned finials or spindles than to make them yourself. Alternatively, you could buy all your gingerbread ornamentation from one of the growing number of millwork manufacturers that produce it. Then, simply finish and install it yourself. However, we assume that most do-it-yourselfers intend to take the more money-saving, practical approach.

Wood Materials

Solid Wood. You will need good wood, but it need not be exceedingly expensive. Cheaper grades are often practical to use for most jobs. With careful layout, you will be able to cut around knots and other defects, eliminating all imperfections. As a rule, use softwoods for exterior projects.

Typical softwood 2 × 4's, 2 × 6's, and similar lumber used in building construction is a good, economical choice as long as it is properly dried. See Illus. 1-1. Avoid freshly cut lumber and most pressure-treated woods for jobs other than in-ground applications, such as posts. Pressure-treated wood that is not properly dried — a common problem — is sure to shrink, distort, and check. And pressure-treated timbers produce sawdust and fumes that are better avoided.

Today's 2 × 4's and 2 × 6's are just 1½ inches in thickness and 3½ and 5½ inches in width, respectively. Make boards wider by gluing narrower ones edge to edge, as shown in Illus. 1-2. Boards sold as 1 inch in thickness are actually ¾ inch

Illus. 1-1. Common softwood construction boards and timbers can be used for making exterior gingerbread as long as they are adequately dried and seasoned.

Illus. 1-2. Gluing two 2 × 6 lengths of Western cedar decking material together edge-to-edge provides wide, heavy material for making exterior brackets.

thick. There is a wide selection of 1-inch material to choose from. Woods such as white fir, pine, basswood, poplar, cedar and oak are all good choices. Let your choice be influenced by the price.

Clear redwood (Illus. 1-3), though very expensive, is very easy to work and it weathers beautifully. You may want to consider it for certain special jobs. Good clear pine is surprisingly expensive and should be avoided because of the cost. Consider using no. 2 pine for small jobs. Use clear cedar, poplar, or basswood where larger knot-free material is required.

You may also want to check the price of mahogany. Some sources claim that certain kinds of mahogany are priced very favorably compared to clear pine and redwood. As a rule, mahogany weathers well. Oak and pine are the standards for a

Illus. 1-3. Some common 1-inch materials include (left to right): clear-heart redwood, which is very expensive, No. 2 pine, poplar, and oak.

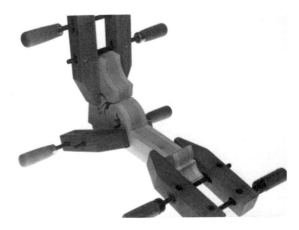

Illus. 1-4. Layers of thinner materials can be glued together face-to-face to make thicker stock. Depending upon the design, it may be better to saw before gluing.

natural indoor finish on most authentic-looking gingerbread, but you should use whatever species you find aesthetic and workable. We have used dark-stained willow to simulate walnut.

Remember that thicker material can be made by gluing two or more layers together, as shown in Illus. 1-4.

Glues (Illus. 1-5). Plastic resin and the new, one-part, ready-to-use waterproof liquid glues just introduced by Tightbond are easy to use and perform very well. Plastic resin comes as a dry powder, which you add water to. Once the resin cures, the joint becomes waterproof. Warm water can be used for cleanup with both kinds of glues before they set.

Panel Materials (Illus. 1-6). Exterior fir plywoods can be used for making certain kinds of brackets, headers and cutouts for other applications. Avoid fir plywoods for interior jobs unless the work will be painted over. Fir plywood is a post-Victorian-era material and is neither appropriate nor authentic. Standard fir plywood splinters easily, has wild grain, and often has voids, or openings within its plies or layers, that become exposed at the edges when cut. Special sealers are available to hide the wild grain, and holes or voids in the plywood edges can be filled, but it's extra work.

Sign painters and some specialty wood-product manufacturers use a specific type of exterior fir plywood that can be used with good results for painted, exterior gingerbread. This special grade is also made with very few voids within its plies, and

Illus. 1-6. Exterior fir plywood can be used for some exterior brackets and panels. Cheaper grades and those not coated with resin-impregnated kraft paper overlays are not as desirable. Note the coating on the two at the right.

Illus. 1-5. For exterior work, use only adhesives that are highly water resistant or, better yet, those that are waterproof.

13

it has resin-impregnated kraft paper covering one or both surfaces. Because of this overlay, it splinters very little and finishes easily. This special plywood is often sold as "Duraply." Building supply centers that don't stock it can order it. We have made many brackets and sign blanks from this material. It is available in ½-inch and ¾-inch thicknesses and can be glued face-to-face to make thicker stock.

Mouldings and Turnings (Illus. 1-7 to 1-10) include many components for making your own gingerbread and give your work a professional look. If you have a router or shaper and the appropriate cutters, you can mill your own mouldings. See page 27. You can also mill or turn your own round components. In fact, with a router, you can even make your own dowels. Refer to the *Router Handbook.*

Usually it is practical to buy your mouldings and spindle turnings. That is, unless you intend to tool up for a large production run or you simply can't find a particular design. In such cases you will have to turn your own or have the job done for you.

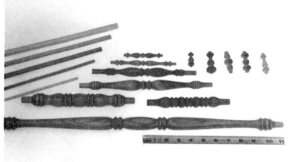

Illus. 1-7. Wood mouldings of many shapes can be purchased or made. See page 27.

Illus. 1-8. Ready-to-use dowels and turnings are available in many sizes and varieties of wood, including birch, oak and cherry, to name a few.

Balls and Beads (Illus. 1-9) are actually special turnings that are available in a variety of sizes and are used for making spandrels and fan brackets. They can be purchased solid or predrilled, and even prefinished. Round wood balls are available in sizes ranging from ⅜ inch to 3 inches in diameter.

Finials (Illus. 1-11 and 1-12) are decorative turnings used to ornament the ends of posts. They point upward at the top of a signpost or can drop downward, as on a corbel or bracket. Finials are seldom positioned horizontally, but they could be. Give careful thought before using them in this unusual position, to assure that the overall design will be visually appropriate.

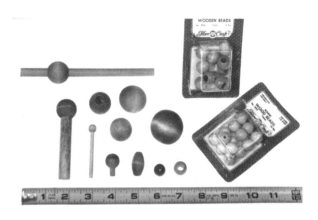

Illus. 1-9. Purchase hardwood dowels and/or beads for making spandrels, fan brackets, and the like. Balls from ⅜ inch to 3 inches in diameter can be purchased at building-supply outlets and by mail order.

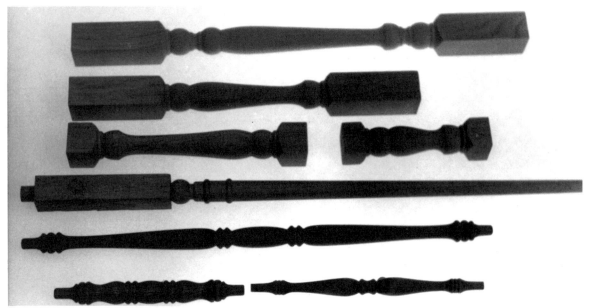

Illus. 1-10. Ready-made large turnings such as these, ranging from 6 inches to several feet in length, are available at building-supply centers. These are used not only for interior applications but for outdoor porch railings as well and for constructing Victorian porch spandrels. See Chapter 9.

Illus. 1-11. A variety of smaller, commercially turned and sanded finials.

Illus. 1-12. Large finials such as these are available to top-off sign and mailbox posts or to use as drops on large corbels and brackets.

2

BASIC LAYOUT TECHNIQUES

This chapter provides an overview of various layout procedures to help inexperienced woodworkers. It begins with some methods of pattern enlargement and offers tips to help do the job better and faster. Layout procedures depend on many things: the style or design of the object to be made, the kind and size of stock, and the quantity of pieces required.

Layout of Patterns. Many patterns in this book can be used at their given size. Consider the size of your home and such things as ceiling or porch heights, headroom clearances, and appearances, to be sure you use patterns that are in fact sized to your specific needs and desires. If you elect not to use the patterns at the sizes given in this book, you will probably want to enlarge them.

Enlarging on the Copy Machine. The fastest, most practical way to make accurate copies is to use a copy machine with enlarging capabilities. Some machines enlarge copies at one-percent increments. Some can make 200-percent enlargements in just one copy.

Grid System. Craftspeople have used this technique for decades to enlarge patterns. Here is the general procedure. First, draw uniformly sized squares on transparent tissue, or scratch the squares on thin, clear plastic. You can also use the grid (Illus. 2-1) and have a transparency (Illus. 2-2) made of it. (Some photocopy machines make transparencies.) Use your tissue (or transparency grid) or draw grid lines over the patterns in the book.

Next, on a piece of paper about the size you want the bracket or other part to be, divide the space into the same number of squares as the pattern under the transpar-

1"GRID

Illus. 2-1. Grid.

Illus. 2-2. Using a transparent grid placed over the original pattern.

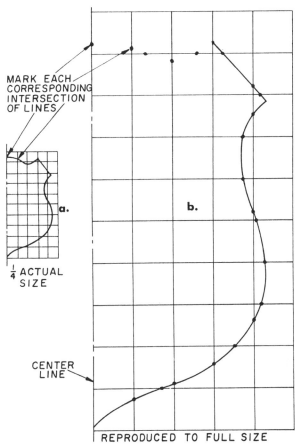

MARK EACH CORRESPONDING INTERSECTION OF LINES

a.

b.

$\frac{1}{4}$ ACTUAL SIZE

CENTER LINE

REPRODUCED TO FULL SIZE

Illus. 2-3. Enlarging and copying a design, square by square. This example has a 1-to-4 ratio, which means the new design is four times larger than the original.

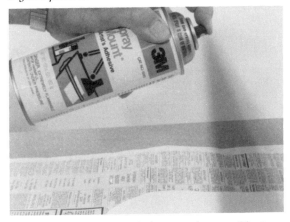

Illus. 2-4. Apply a very light mist of spray adhesive to the back of the pattern only. Do not spray directly onto the wood. A newspaper catches the overspray.

ency has. The actual size of the larger set of squares will be determined by the enlargement ratio desired. For example, if you want the design twice the size of the original, draw the new squares double the size of the ones on the original pattern.

Now, copy the pattern square by square. Copy each point of the original pattern onto the graph squares. Draw the curves by "eye" after plotting their direction with reference to the surrounding square. See Illus. 2-3.

Once you have drawn the pattern you can apply it temporarily to the work with rubber cement or spray adhesive. See Illus. 2-4 and 2-5. You can also transfer the pattern profile using carbon or graphite paper (the latter is cleaner). We recommend spray adhesive for accuracy and convenience. Apply a very light mist to the back of the paper pattern only. Wait a few seconds until the adhesive is tacky, and press it onto the wood. One kind of temporary bonding adhesive that works well is 3-M's Scotch Spray Mount Artist's Adhesive #6065, but other brands work well. Always test the adhesive on a small sample first.

Illus. 2-5. Pressing the spray-adhesive-coated copy of the pattern directly onto the wood blank.

Illus. 2-6. After the profile has been cut out, the pattern will peel off the wood cleanly and easily.

Illus. 2-7. Plan your layouts to save material. Here one rectangular panel provides minimal waste when making this pair of sawn brackets.

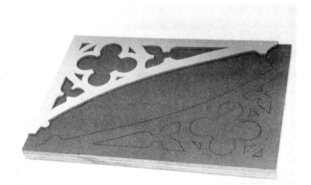

Illus. 2-8. Making multiple layouts by tracing around a thin template.

After the sawing or other machining is completed, peel the pattern off the wood, leaving no residue on the surface. See Illus. 2-6.

Templates are permanent patterns made from thin cardboard, hardboard, plastic, or plywood. See Illus. 2-7 and 2-8. A template can be cut independently or can be sawn at the same time as the project. Simply attach the template material above, below, or in between layers of your wood stock with tape, glue, or nails.

Grain Direction. Consider this carefully to minimize waste. See Illus. 2-7–2-9. As a rule, when working with solid wood, place your patterns on the board so that their longest distance (dimension) is in line with the grain of the wood. A typical example is shown in Illus. 2-9. This provides the best overall strength to the part.

Illus. 2-9. For strength, to minimize short grain, and to conserve material, lay out patterns obliquely to the grain, as shown.

For example, if a bracket is to have square, straight sides as an outside corner, square that corner of the wood before transferring the pattern to it, so those two sides will need no further cutting. See Illus. 2-10.

Think ahead. Nestle parts in the layout to conserve material whenever possible. Inspect both sides of your wood to be sure they are defect-free before laying out the work. Also think about how you plan to cut inside areas. Perfectly round openings are often best cut with a boring-tool process rather than a saw. Locate hole centers and employ "turning hole" strategy when sharp inside curves need to be sawn. See Illus. 2-10 and refer to Illus. 3-8 and 3-9.

Finally, consider using multiple-sawing or -boring operations — in other words, stacking several pieces on top of one another and drilling or sawing them all at the same time.

Illus. 2-10. Sharp, inside curves are often best drilled or bored rather than sawn with wide blades. Note that the pattern is laid out against the presquared corner of the material.

TOOL PROCESSES

This chapter covers techniques that pertain specifically to procedures involved in making Victorian gingerbread.

The tools or machines needed to construct any particular gingerbread project will vary depending upon the design and size (thickness) of the part in question. The best way to do any job will also depend upon how your shop is equipped. If you're going into production, you will want to use more than just a coping saw. A coping saw can cut brackets and many other parts but with less speed and accuracy than other methods.

It's good to have a variety of hand tools. These should include a pencil, square, hammer, plane, and a rasp, some clamps, a chisel, caulking gun, putty knife, and a nail set. You will also need finishing tools, such as sandpaper and brushes. A hand-held electric drill and a hand-held sabre/jig saw are great if a drill press and scroll and band-sawing machines are not available. Commercially available cutters and jigs are shown in this chapter. They are very helpful, but not essential.

Safety. You should by all means observe proper safety practices with your tools and equipment. Many books and other publications provide this information. Alternatively, you can enlist the guidance of a professional teacher-woodworker.

The order in which different operations are performed depends entirely on the nature of the design, the kind and thickness of the wood and the number of items to be made. Sometimes it is best to drill and bore holes before sawing. Other jobs will be best accomplished by sawing first and then making holes.

Drilling and Boring. These jobs are important operations and are done frequently when making gingerbread. Drilling refers to making holes ½ inch in

diameter and smaller; boring means making holes larger than ½ inch in diameter. See Illus. 3-1 and 3-2. Drilling and boring are best done on a drill press (Illus. 3-3), but for many gingerbread jobs a drill press is not really essential.

Illus. 3-2. Boring large holes through two layers of ³/₄-inch "Duraply" plywood with a multi-spur bit. These large holes comprise part of the pattern's profile or its design shape.

Illus. 3-1. Drilling through a round ball. A "V"-grooved block is secured to the drill-press table with double-faced tape. This simple fixture assures that all holes will be centered exactly every time.

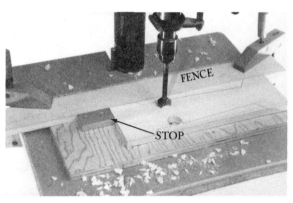

Illus. 3-3. Production setup for boring large holes when making sawn porch balusters. Rather than saw the inside curve of the profile, it is cut by this boring operation. Note the fence clamped to the table and the stop used to position all subsequent pieces identically without measuring.

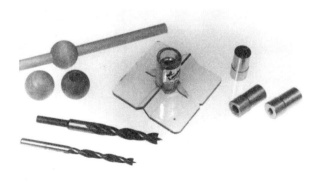

Illus. 3-4. An inexpensive and helpful guide for free-hand drilling without a drill press. It has several different-size steel bushings. Use this guide to make perpendicular holes on flat surfaces and cylinders and to drill center holes in wood balls. Note the brad-point bits that are best for clean, accurate drilling.

Illus. 3-4 shows a small, inexpensive, plastic drilling jig that can be used with an electric hand drill to drill holes that are perpendicular to flat and curved surfaces. You can automatically drill perpendicularly into dowels and automatically center-drill into wood balls (Illus. 3-5). Automatically centering a hole in the edge of a board can be done perfectly with the help of a dowel jig. This jig clamps to thick or thin boards while automatically centering itself. Once clamped in the correct position, it guides the drill bit straight and true. See Illus. 3-6 and 3-7.

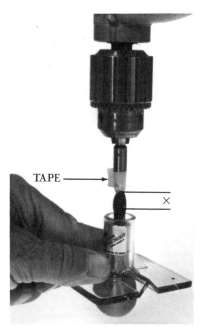

Illus. 3-5. Using the guide to drill into the center of a wood ball. Notice the tape on the bit used to indicate when the proper depth, "X," is achieved.

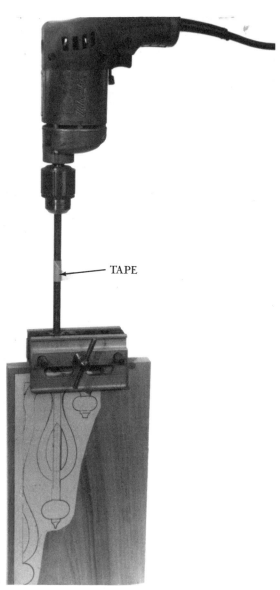

Illus. 3-7. Using a dowel-drilling jig to center and guide the bit for drilling a very deep hole in a bracket before sawing it out. The tape on the bit indicates when the desired hole depth is reached.

Illus. 3-6. A dowel-drilling jig and special long bits are helpful for some projects.

Sawing. The best sawing tool to use depends upon four basic considerations: (1) the overall size of the stock; (2) whether the line will be straight or curved; (3) the thickness of the material; and (4) if the line will be curved, the sharpness or radius of the curve. (This assumes the piece is large enough to saw safely.)

For straight-line sawing use these tools in descending order of preference: (a) table or radial saw, (b) electric hand-held circular saw, (c) band saw, (d) handsaw, and (e) portable electric jig/scroll saw.

Use the band saw to cut curves in thick material. Employ a "turning hole" technique for making sharp, inside curves. See Illus. 3-8. In this technique the sharply curved edge is made by a drilling or boring technique and is not actually cut with the saw blade at all. Illustrations 3-8 and 3-9 show how the technique works.

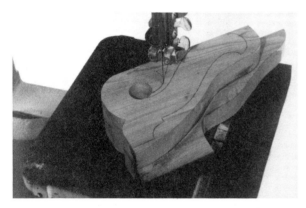

Illus. 3-8. Use a band saw to cut thick or stacked (layered) material. This illustration shows sawing into a "turning hole" previously bored to form part of the sharply curved line so it need not be cut with the saw, which would have twisted the blade.

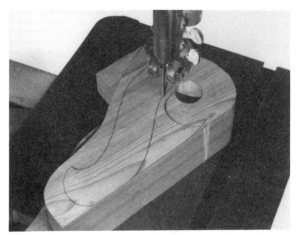

Illus. 3-9. After sawing into the "turning hole," continue cutting the line by sawing out from it.

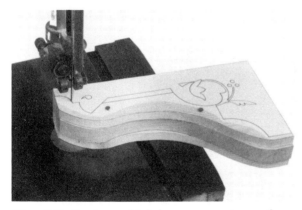

Illus. 3-10. Sawing multiple layers at once is a good job for the band saw.

Illus. 3-11. With appropriate blades, a hand-held electric jig saw can be used to cut out many sawn ornaments.

Band saws are great for stack sawing many layers at once. Illus. 3-10 shows three bracket layers nailed together and sawn all at one time. If you don't have a band saw you may need to make thick objects from two or more thinner boards glued together after each piece is cut out separately.

Thinner stock can be sawn very nicely with the hand-held electric jig/scroll saw shown in Illus. 3-11 and 3-12. Most hand-held jig/scroll saw work must be clamped to a workbench or table with the cutting area positioned beyond the edge. See Illus. 3-13.

Illus. 3-12. Drilled "turning holes." Sharp curves are also best made by drilling holes so that part of the hole's circumference matches the desired line of cut.

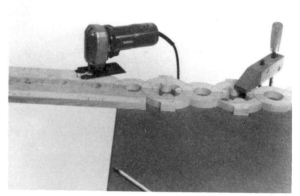

Illus. 3-13. Setup for sawing a mailbox-post grille from ¾-inch solid pine.

Very sharply curved work is best sawn with one of the new constant-tension scroll saw machines. See Illus. 3-14. Some brands of scroll saws are not as effective at cutting certain materials such as plywood and do not make good cuts in thick stock.

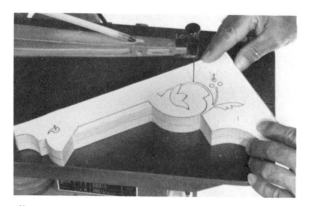

Illus. 3-14. Scroll-saw cutting. Whenever possible, stack two or more layers and saw them at the same time. Note that the nails in the areas to be drilled hold the two layers together for sawing.

Illus. 3-15. Scroll-saw blades suitable for making sharply curved cuts in thick wood. Blades are shown full size.

Cutting 1½-inch plywood, for example, requires a lot of blade tension and sharp blades. Always use the widest blade (Illus. 3-15) possible to minimize breaking. See Illus. 3-16.

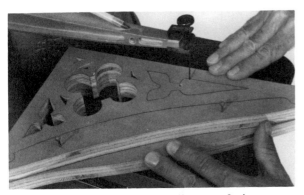

Illus. 3-16. A good saw with a well-tensioned sharp, heavy blade permits accurate sawing of these two layers of ¾-inch-thick exterior plywood brackets.

Illus. 3-17. Use a rasp or wood file to smooth edges cut by a hand-held sabre/scroll saw and those surfaces that were cut by the band saw.

Smoothing and Sanding will depend on how the pieces are prepared, how sawn, and the degree of smoothness desired. Basically, exterior fretwork, which is always painted, does not need to be glass-smooth. It should be worked enough so it looks good. Interior fretwork is another story. If it is to have a natural or stained finish, the smoother the better.

Edges cut with the hand-held, electric scroll/jig saw and the band saw will be much rougher than those cut with a scroll saw. Exterior pieces to be painted can be worked with a rasp and coarse-sanded. See Illus. 3-17. Inside curves can be smoothed with a drum-sanding attachment in the drill press, as shown in Illus. 3-18 and 3-19. Always use the biggest drum size possible to get the smoothest flowing curves.

Illus. 3-18. Drum sanding in a drill press.

Illus. 3-19. Round holes require less sanding if they are made by drilling or boring than by sawing. Sawn holes require careful sanding to a sharp layout line.

Outside or convex curves are, as a rule, sanded or smoothed more easily than inside curves. Do not use drum sanders for this work. The disc sander shown in Illus. 3-20 is easy to make and works well on many sanding jobs. The disc is just a piece of flat plywood. The abrasive is glued to it with a temporary bond-type spray adhesive. The disc is mounted on a nifty, inexpensive arbor available at most hardware stores. It will probably be necessary to shim the drill slightly in the drill stand or at the base to make the surface of the abrasive disc run at 90 degrees to the table.

Routing and Shaping are jobs for the serious woodworker. If you don't have a router or similar equipment you can often revise the plan or the pattern to eliminate those tasks.

A hand-held router is a great advantage if you know how to use it. It allows you to round over, cove, and bevel (chamfer) edges of mouldings, frames, and brackets. See Illus. 3-21 through 3-23. Numerous special bits are available to allow you to

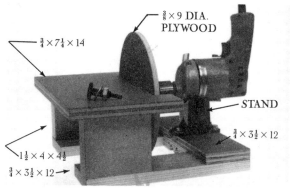

Illus. 3-20. This shop-made, electric-drill-driven disc sander will smooth outside (convex) curves quickly and easily. An arbor (as shown on the table) and a plastic drill-stand clamp (optional) are purchased components.

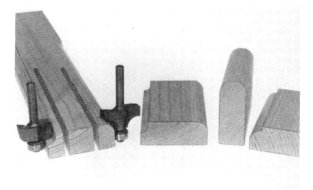

Illus. 3-21. With these basic bits you can create many different mouldings and decorative edges.

Illus. 3-22. Making a cove cut along an edge.

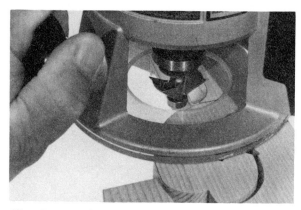

Illus. 3-23. A close-up look at routing a chamfer along the edge of a thick bracket.

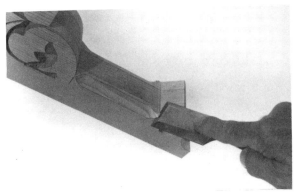

Illus. 3-24. Use a sharp chisel to finish off the ends of a routed chamfer cut.

Illus. 3-25. Routing flutes along a curved inside edge of a bracket.

Illus. 3-26. Routing flutes to uniform depths along an outside curve on this thick corbel. Note the test piece above used to check the spacings between flutes.

Illus. 3-27. A plunge router, fitted with an edge guide-fence, cuts slots in 2 × 4's. The pieces will receive the grillework for Victorian mailbox posts. (See page 165.)

Illus. 3-28. This router-table operation cuts a decorative cove around dowel ends. The dowel is held against a block (board) that is clamped to the router table. The operator carefully rotates the dowel against the rotation of the bit to complete this shaping cut.

Illus. 3-29. The new "super" glues are great for this kind of ball-to-dowel gluing job and for many other gingerbread-fretwork assemblies.

reproduce any existing shape or to make interesting new cuts when creating your own gingerbread decorations. For example, piloted-grooving and flute-cutting bits are available in various sizes to produce interesting forward edges on thick brackets and corbels. See Illus. 3-25 and 3-26. The ball-bearing pilot at the end of the bit controls the horizontal depth of cut. This results in perfect, uniformly cut flutes cut into the edges of inside and outside curves or along straight surfaces.

Grooves or mortise-type slots in frame work designed to receive grilles or inset brackets can be cut perfectly with a plunge-type router, as shown in Illus. 3-27. With a router and a router table, you can make decorative dowel ends, as shown in Illus. 3-28. See *Router Basics* and *Router Handbook* for more information about routers and bits.

Assembly Techniques for decorative gingerbread projects generally involve gluing, nailing, using wood screws, or a combination of these processes. Use waterproof glues for all exterior jobs. Refer to Illus. 1-5, page 13. Non-corrosive metal fasteners are also a good choice. Interior assembly should focus on the appearance of the piece more than anything else. The new "super glues" (Illus. 3-29) are worth trying for many interior jobs. They are good to use on work that will be given a natural finish. Slight glue squeeze-outs are not at all visible. If you are nailing pieces together, be sure to set all nails below the surfaces and fill all of the nail holes. See Illus. 3-30 and 3-31.

Illus. 3-30. Toe nailing a sawn bracket into place. Here, a hole is first made with the hand drill to minimize any chance of splitting. Incidentally, the "bit" is actually a finishing nail with its head cut off.

Illus. 3-31. Using small brads to fasten mitred cove moulding to a large corbel. It's best to set all nails below the surface and fill the holes.

4

FLAT, SAWN BRACKETS

Brackets are used to decorate squared or framed openings. They are one of the easiest and most popular ways to achieve a Victorian look. There are more general uses for brackets and more places to put them than for just about any other form of gingerbread fretwork. Of the various kinds of brackets (fan brackets and corbels), those sawn from a single thickness are the most popular and easiest for all wood-workers to make themselves.

In most cases, brackets can be made either with or without side frames. This offers two design options and different possibilities for utilizing a single bracket pattern. See Illus. 4-1. There are also different ways in which the optional side frames can be made. Frame edges can be formed or shaped with a router or shaper. In such cases the corner joint, where the two side-frame pieces meet, must be mitred, as shown in Illus. 4-2.

Illus. 4-2. Sawn brackets can be framed in a variety of ways. Left: a routed frame, which requires a mitred corner joint. Right: a square-edge frame material with a simple butt joint.

Illus. 4-1. The bracket on the left is designed with an integral sawn frame. The one on the right has a frame attached to the bracket.

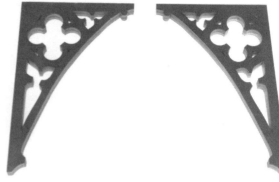

Illus. 4-3. Brackets of unequal widths and lengths can be positioned horizontally, or vertically as shown in Illus. 4-4.

Illus. 4-4.

Various situations may dictate exactly how a bracket is to be installed into a corner or opening. Space restrictions, horizontally for distance and vertically because of head-room clearances or ceiling heights, must be considered. Most brackets can be installed in either of two ways: with the longest leg of the bracket in either a horizontal or in a vertical position. See Illus. 4-3 and 4-4.

Brackets make excellent shelf and mantel supports. Refer to Chapter 6 for some ideas about how to make shelves using many of the bracket patterns provided later in this chapter. The Victorian signpost (Chapter 18), the Victorian mailbox (Chapter 17), screen doors (Illus. 4-5, and Chapter 15), porches, and entrances all involve the use of brackets. You will find many uses for brackets in both small and larger sizes.

Illus. 4-5. This entrance, designed and built by Grant Lanceleve, features brackets in the opening and within the screen door. Refer to Illus. 4-20 for the entrance-bracket pattern.

Illus. 4-7. This frameless bracket is popular on screen doors but can be used in other places.

Illus. 4-6. Another of the many uses for bracket patterns is to decorate stair stringers, as shown here. See Illus. 4-26 for this pattern.

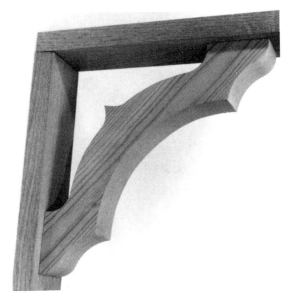

Illus. 4-8. The same bracket with a frame.

Note: Many bracket patterns that follow are half the size of authentic Victorian gingerbread. Many of these patterns are better suited to modern-day homes than the originals would be, because ceilings are much lower now than in Victorian homes. Many shelf-bracket patterns are usable exactly as they appear here. Some patterns have been reduced because of space restraints in this book. However, any pattern can be enlarged (or reduced) easily (see page 17). Do not overlook any pattern because the size you first see may not be the one you need.

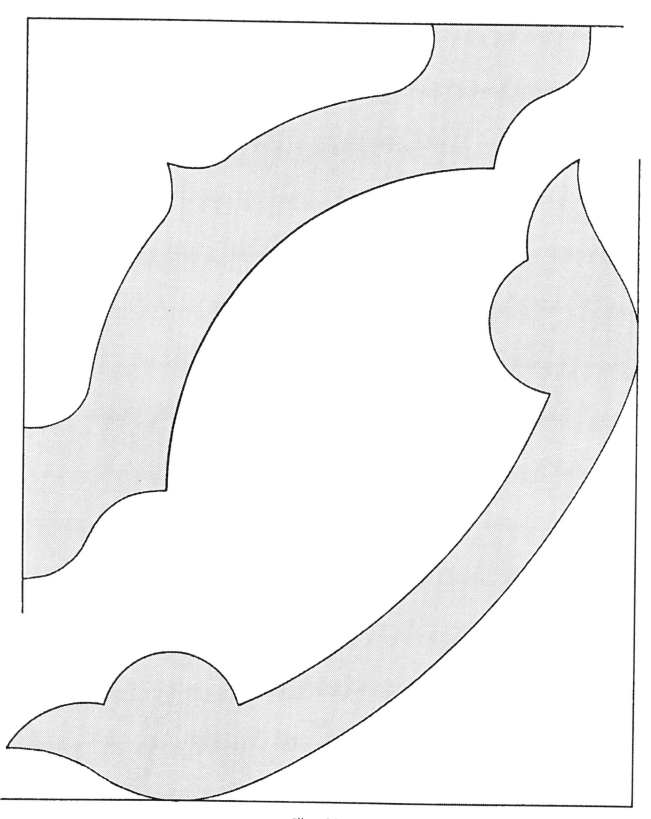

Illus. 4-9.

Illus. 4-10.

Illus. 4-11. Scroll bracket with side frames.

Illus. 4-12.

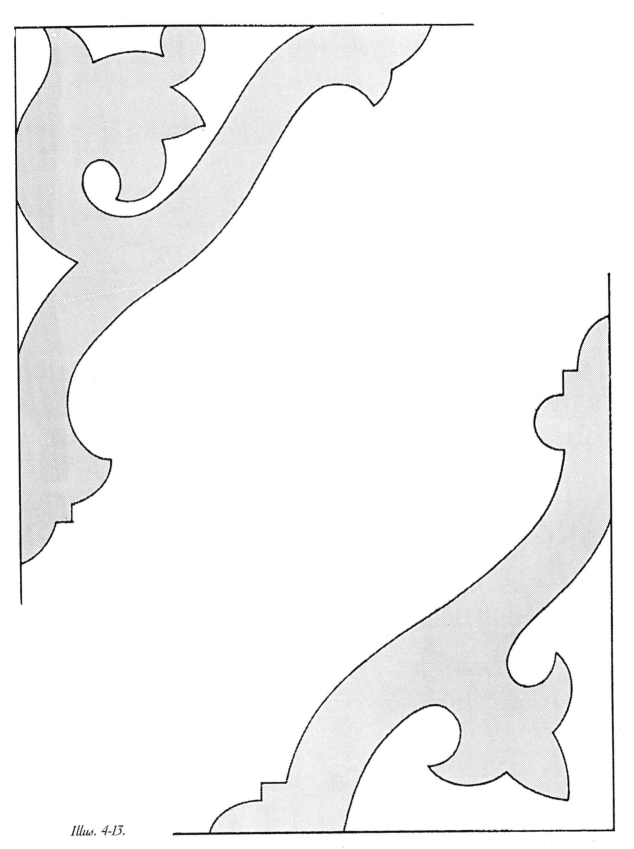

Illus. 4-13.

Illus. 4-14.

Illus. 4-15.

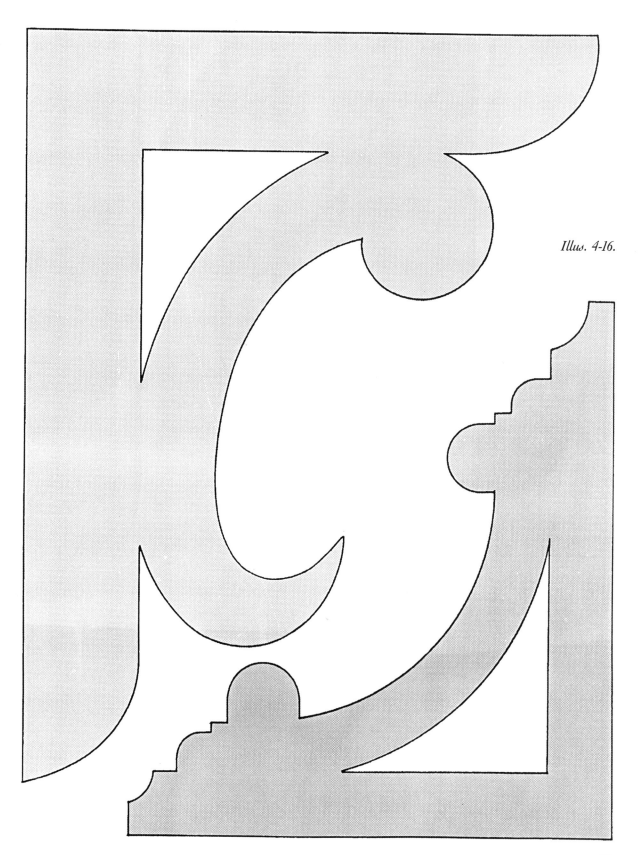

Illus. 4-16.

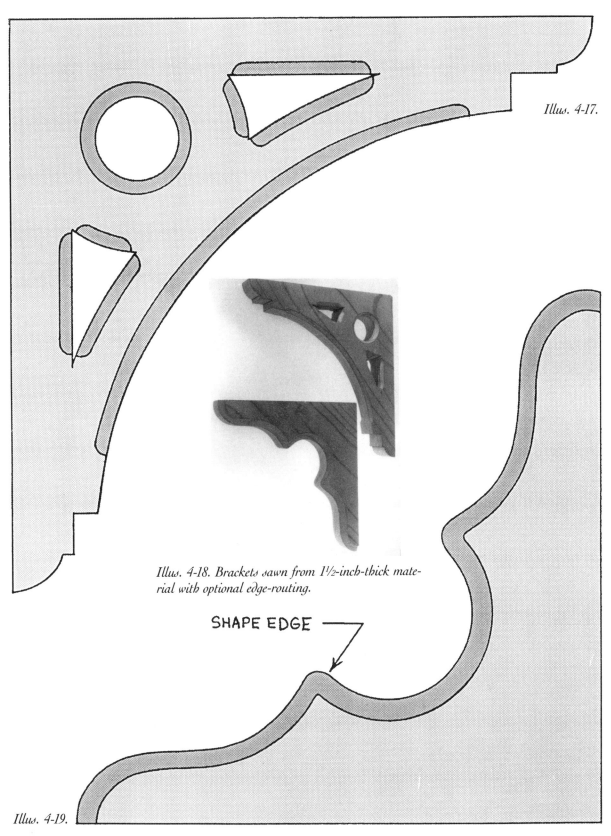

Illus. 4-18. Brackets sawn from 1½-inch-thick mate-rial with optional edge-routing.

SHAPE EDGE

Illus. 4-19.

Illus. 4-20. Patterns courtesy of Grant Lanceleve.

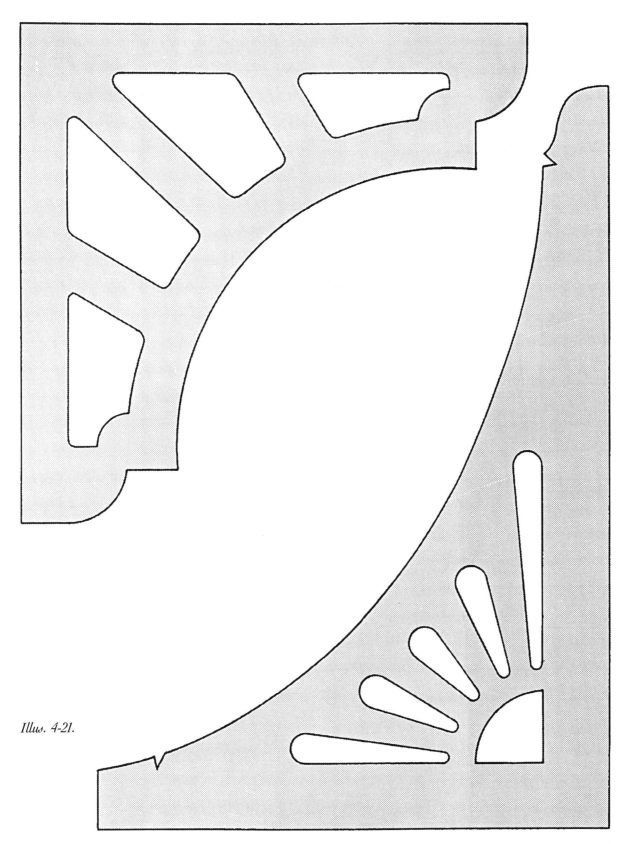

Illus. 4-21.

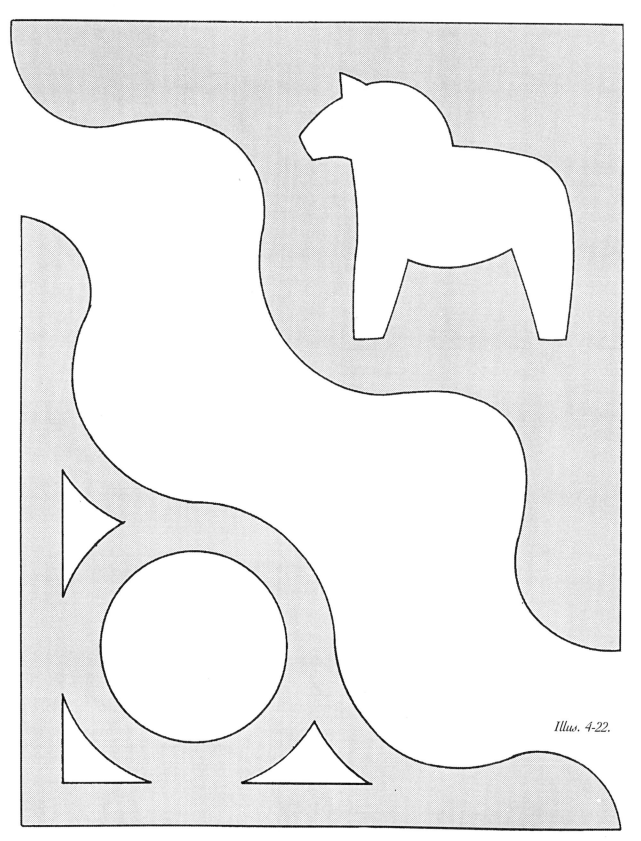

Illus. 4-22.

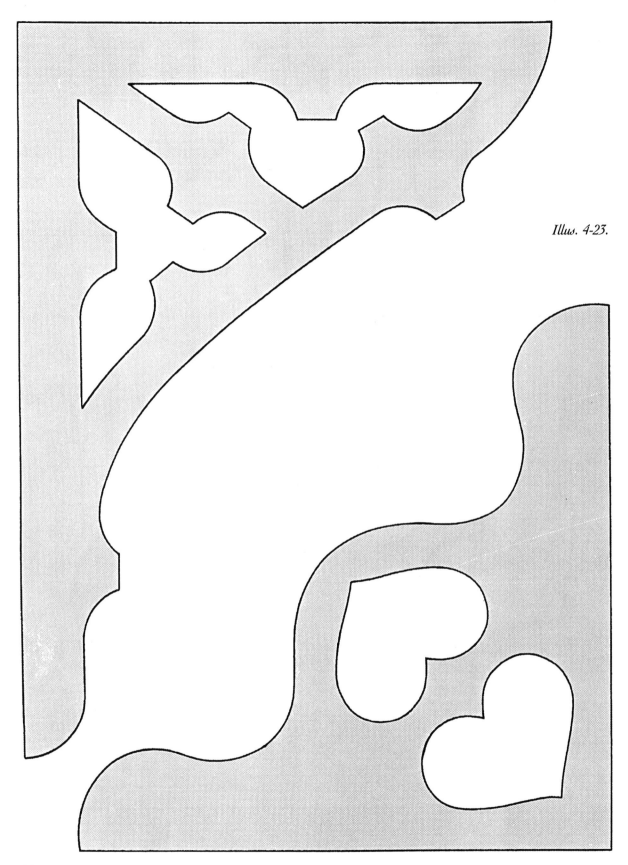

Illus. 4-23.

44

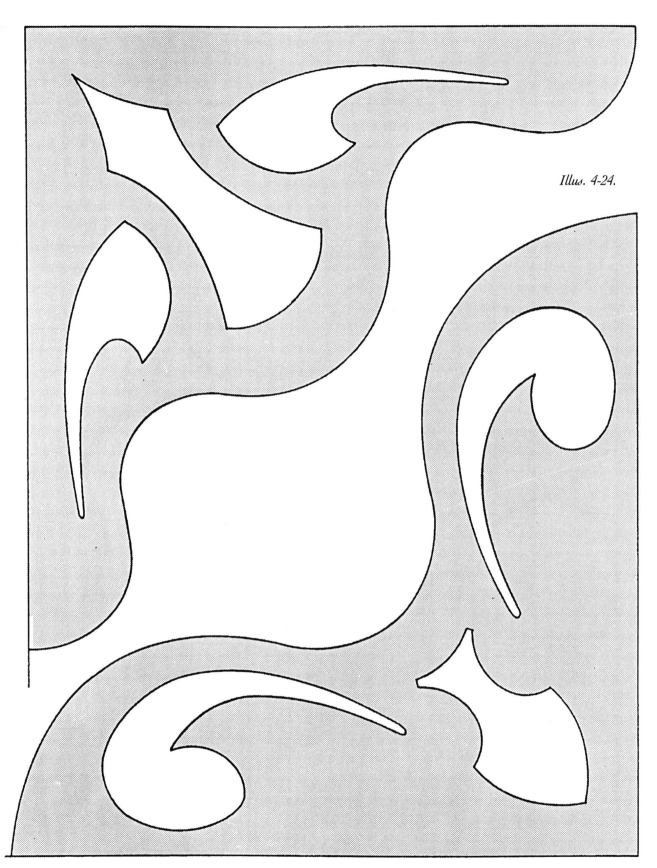

Illus. 4-24.

Illus. 4-25.

Illus. 4-27.

Illus. 4-28.

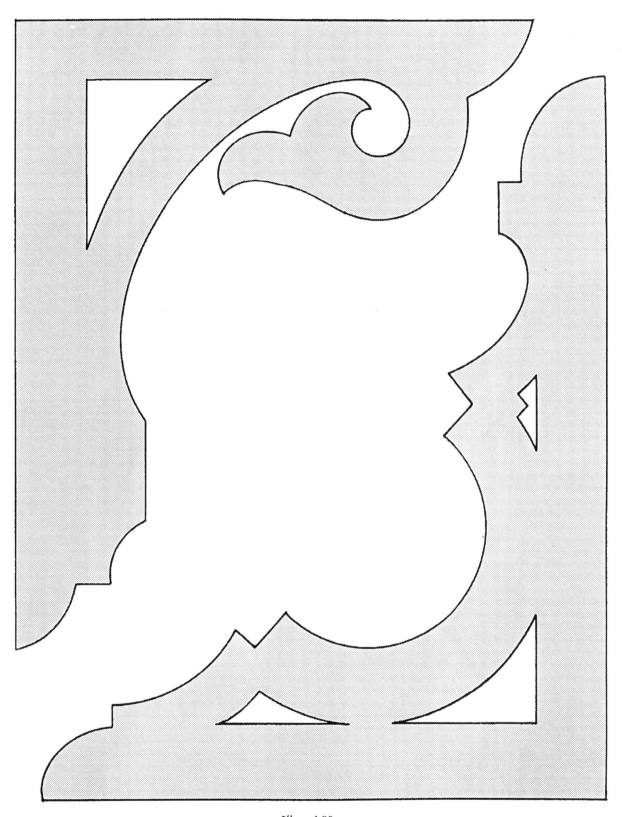

Illus. 4-29.

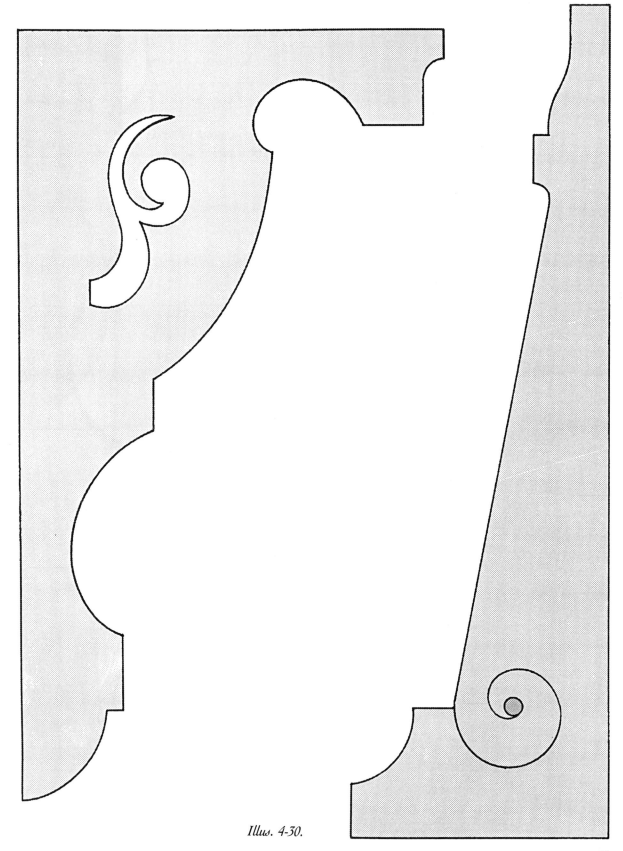

Illus. 4-30.

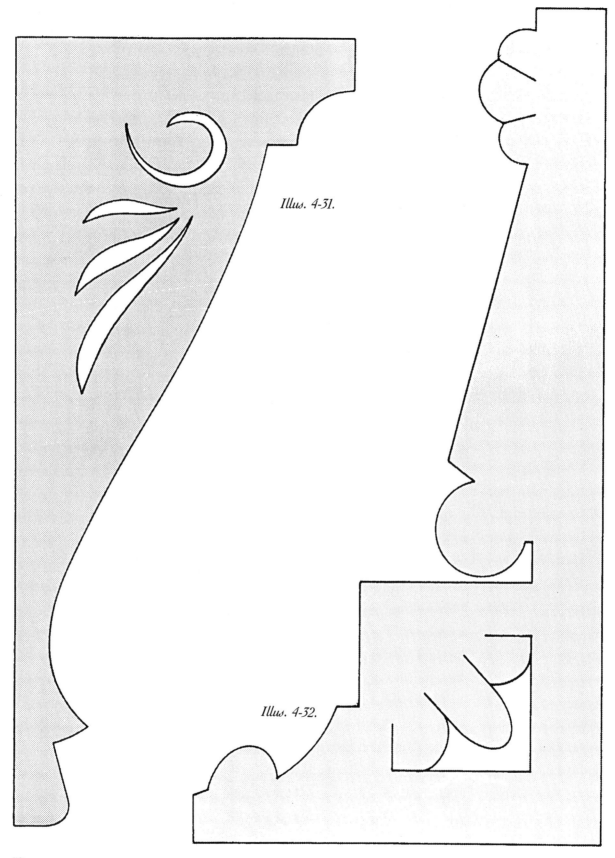

Illus. 4-31.

Illus. 4-32.

Illus. 4-33.

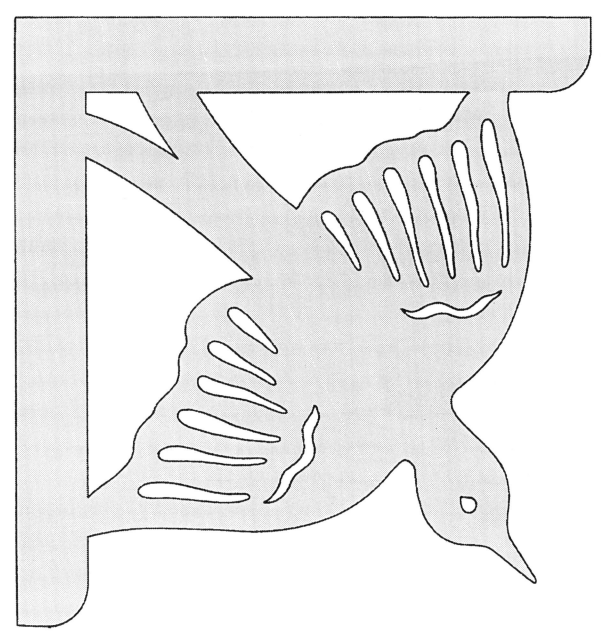

Illus. 4-34.

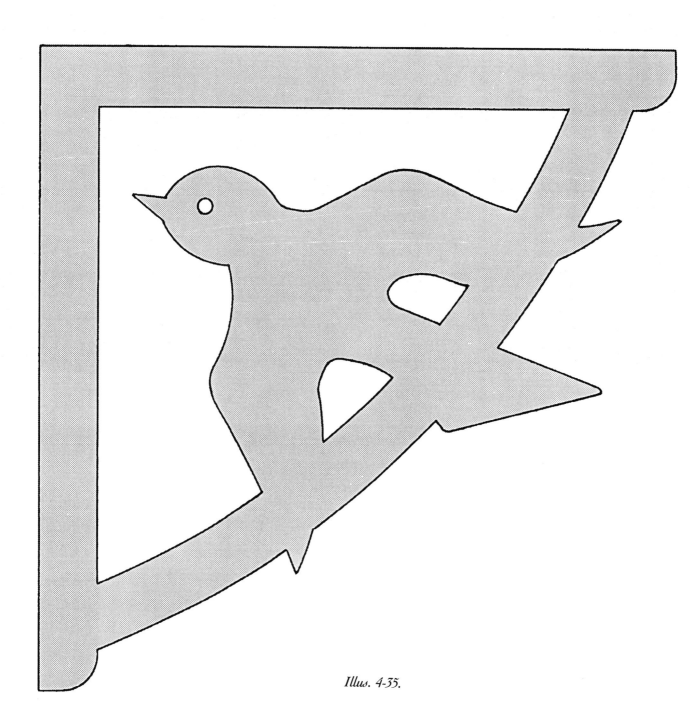

Illus. 4-35.

Illus. 4-36.

Illus. 4-37.

Illus. 4-38.

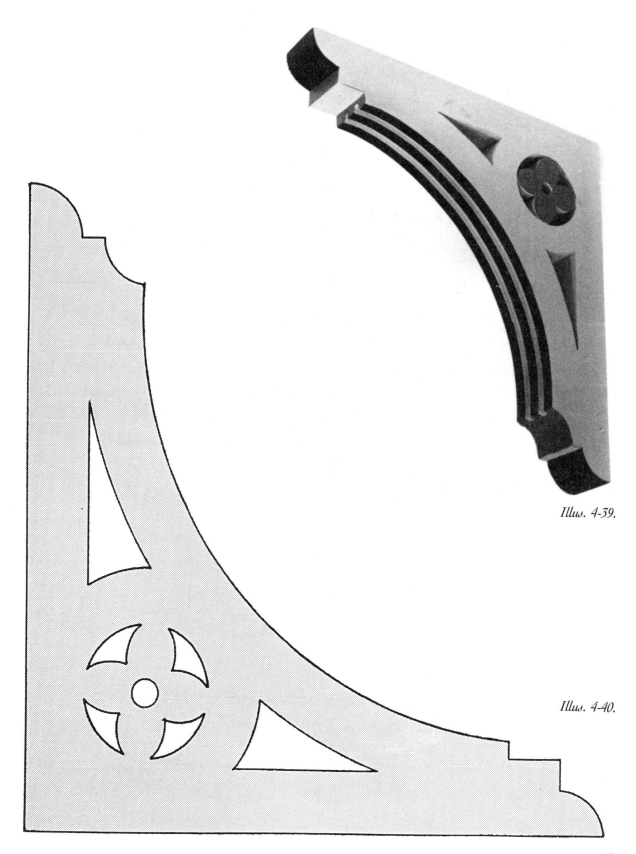

Illus. 4-39.

Illus. 4-40.

59

Illus. 4-41.

Illus. 4-42.

Illus. 4-43.

Illus. 4-44.

Illus. 4-45.

Illus. 4-46.

Illus. 4-47.

Another large corbel used as an indoor shelf measures 7 × 10 × 16 inches .

This large corbel measuring 7½ × 12 × 16 inches is being used indoors as a shelf.

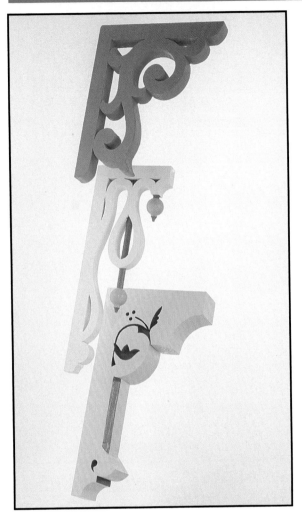

Painted brackets.

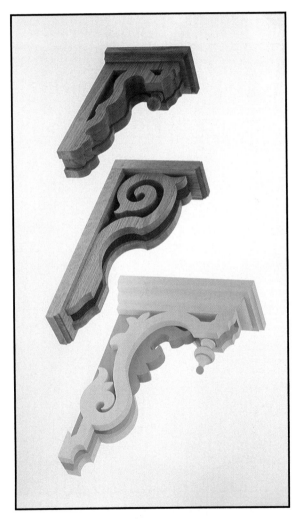

Assortment of smaller corbels.

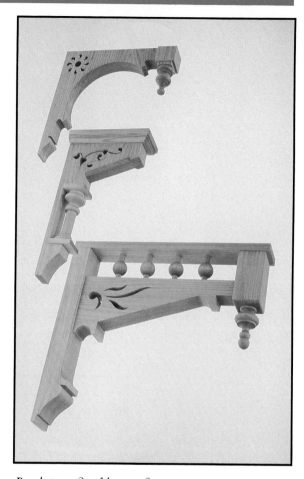

Brackets made of basswood.

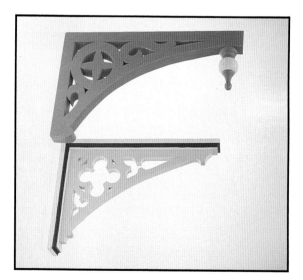

Painted gingerbread brackets.

C

Victorian shelf.

Victorian signs.

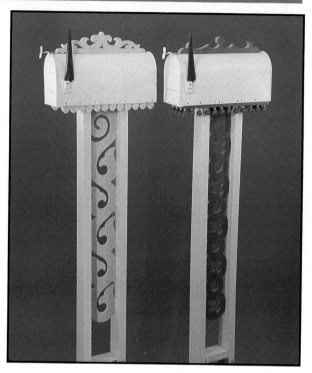

Ornamental mailbox posts. Note the use of headers attached to the tops of the mailboxes.

Victorian gingerbread mailbox post.

Some headers.

Mailbox post brackets.

Interesting details in this modern Victorian boxed bay window. Note the use of corbel-type brackets, circular butt shingles, and the pleasing color combinations.

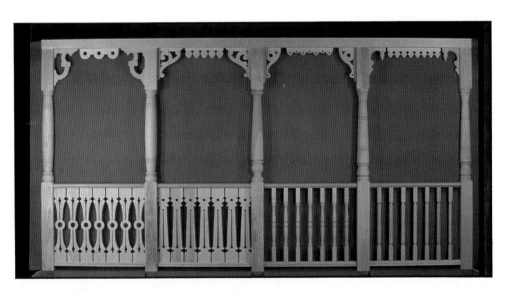

Exterior gingerbread combinations of various brackets, continuous trim, and sawn and turned balusters, with railings and turned posts. (Photo courtesy of Silverton Millworks, Durango, Colorado)

F

A close look at some gable trim fabricated and installed by Grant Lanceleve.

Window planter boxes in the Victorian style designed and crafted by Grant Lanceleve.

Screen door and entrance ornamentation created by Grant Lanceleve.

*Reconstructed home makes good use
of Victorian gingerbread.*

Gingerbread spandrels and brackets at an entrance.

Illus. 4-48.

Illus. 4-49.

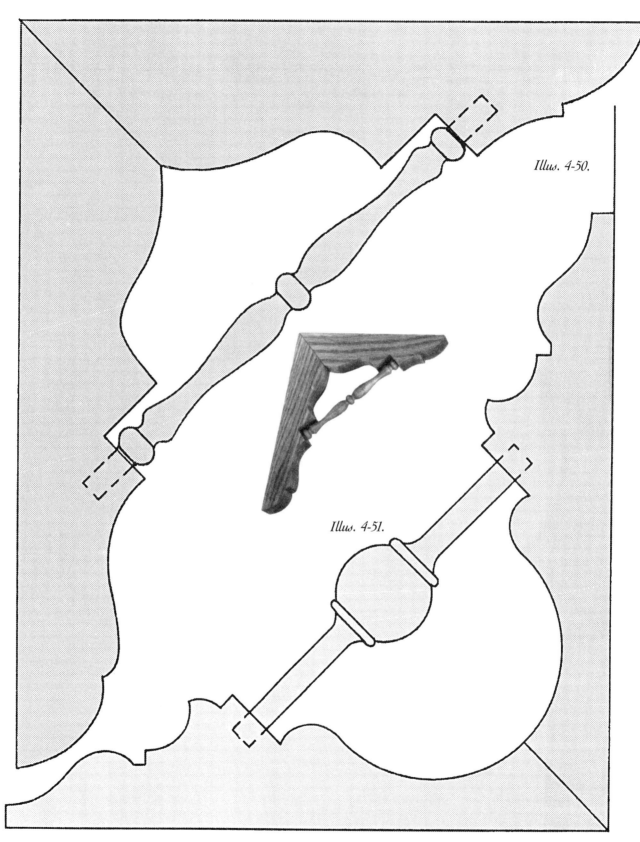

Illus. 4-50.

Illus. 4-51.

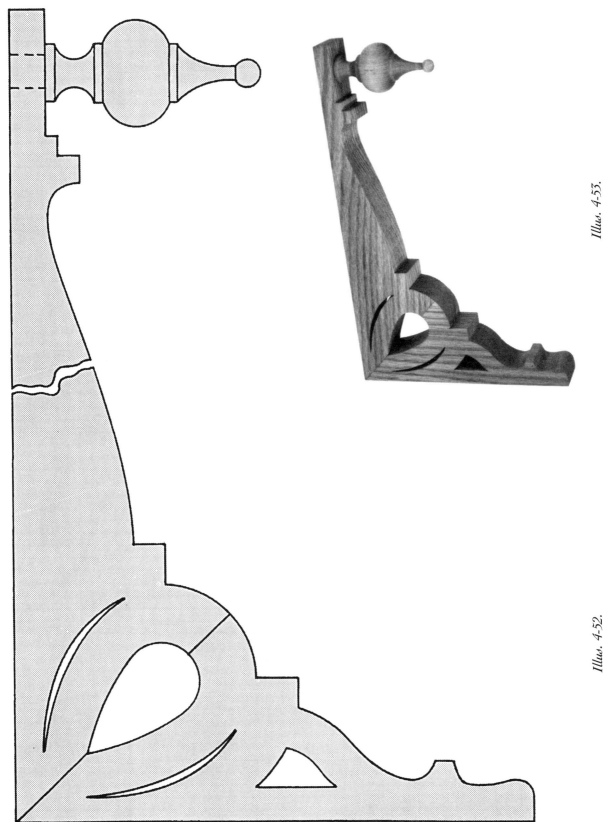

Илл. 4-53.

Илл. 4-52.

68

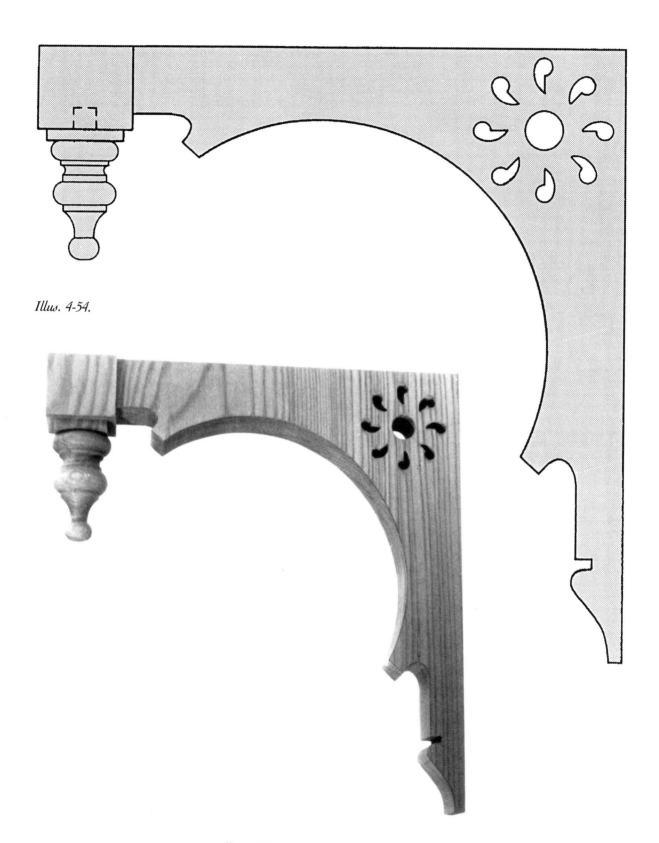

Illus. 4-54.

Illus. 4-55.

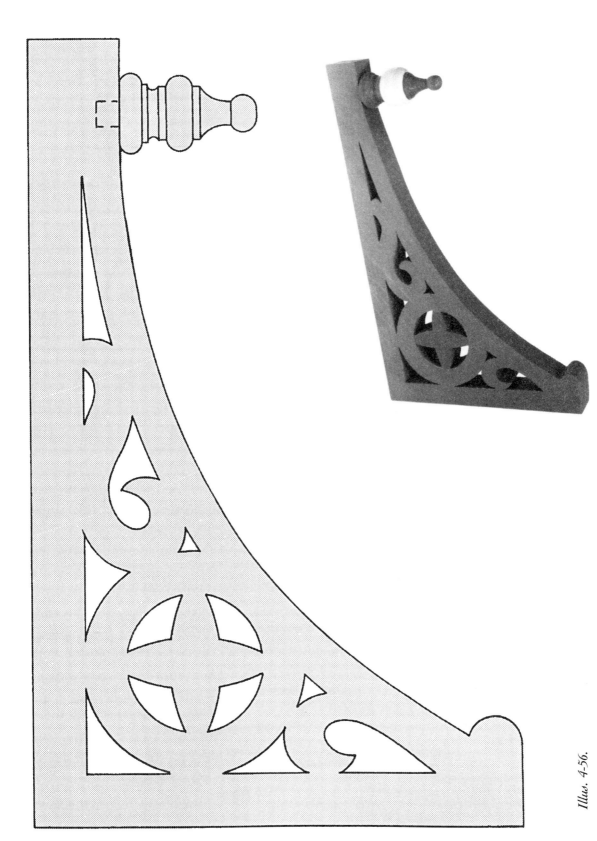

Illus. 4-57.

Illus. 4-56.

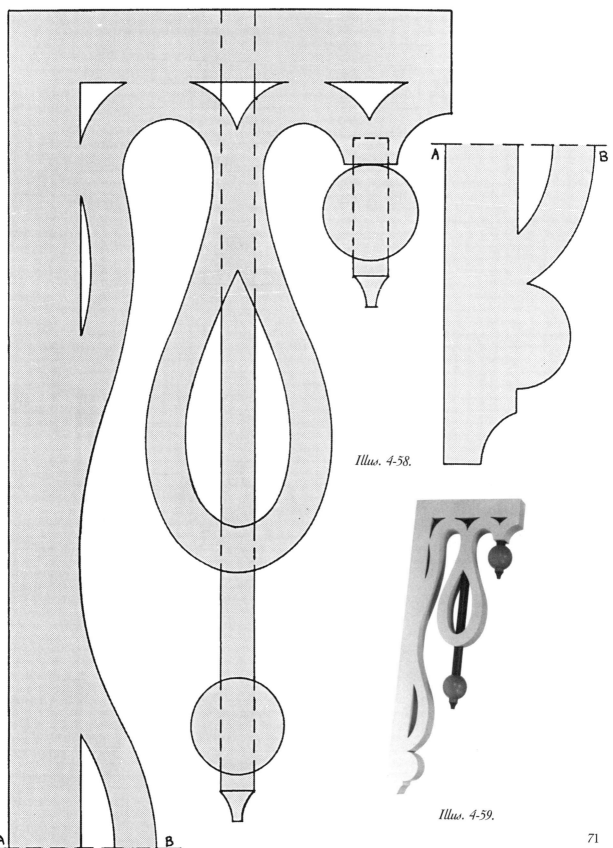

A   B

Illus. 4-58.

A   B

Illus. 4-59.

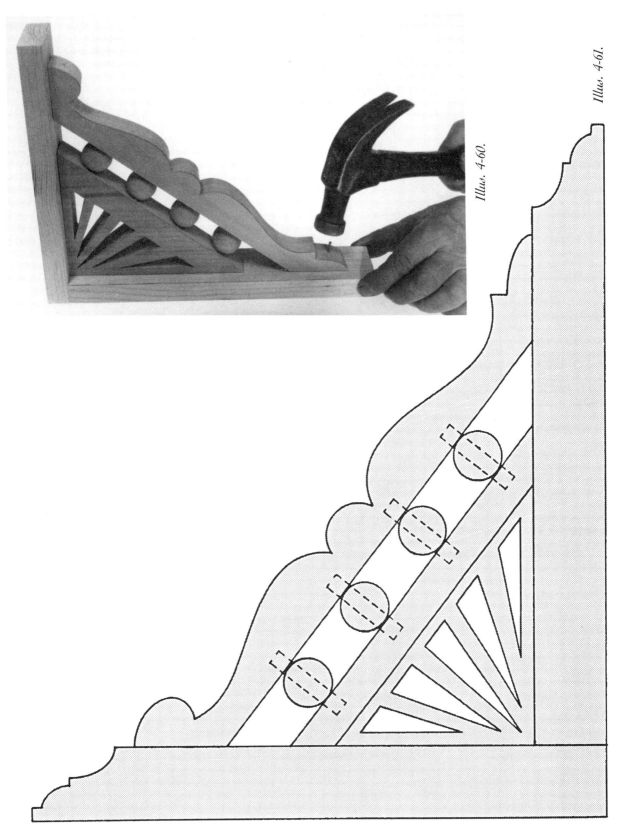

Илл. 4-60.

Илл. 4-61.

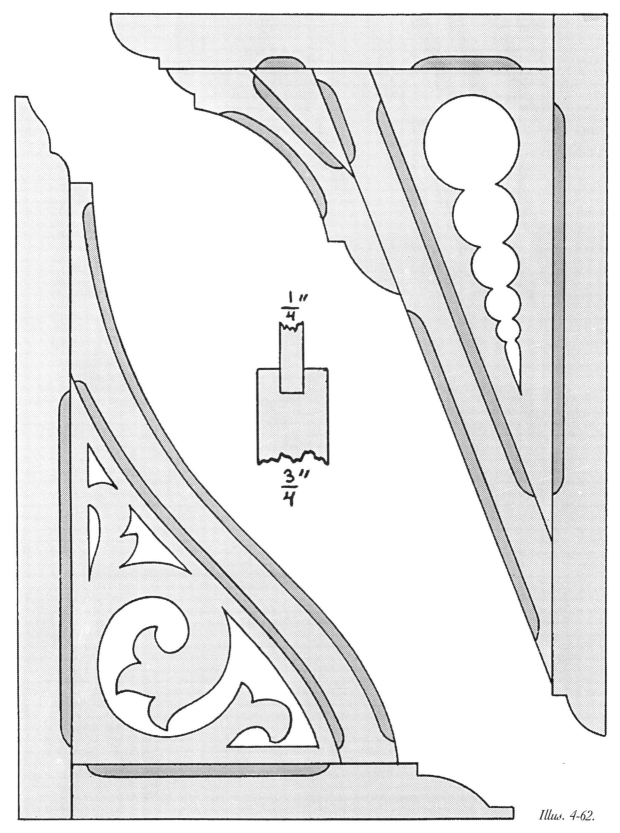

$\frac{1}{4}''$

$\frac{3}{4}''$

Illus. 4-62.

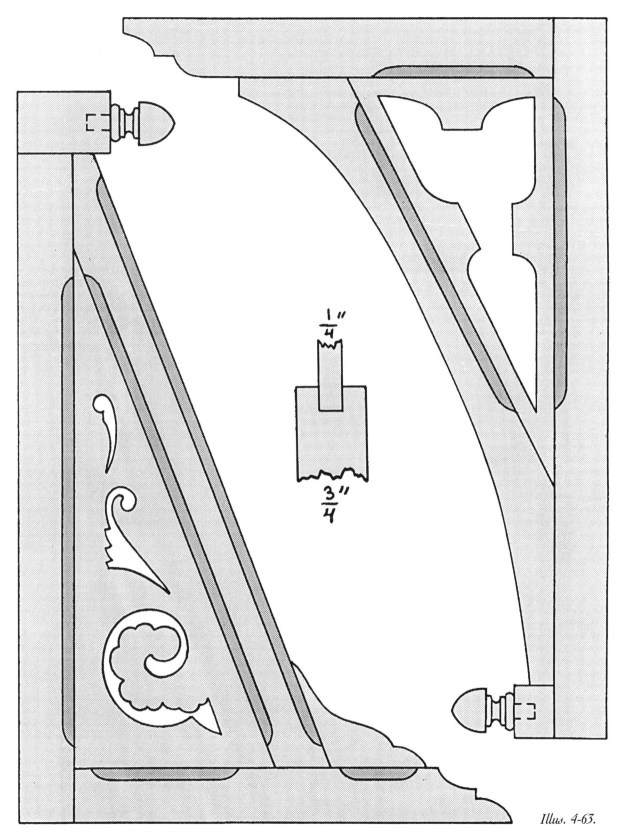

$\frac{1''}{4}$

$\frac{3''}{4}$

Illus. 4-63.

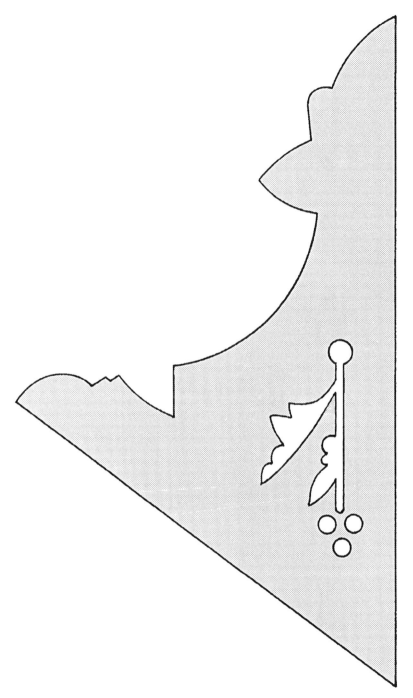

Illus. 4-64. Angle brackets are used under eaves. Modify the included angle to accommodate different roof pitches.

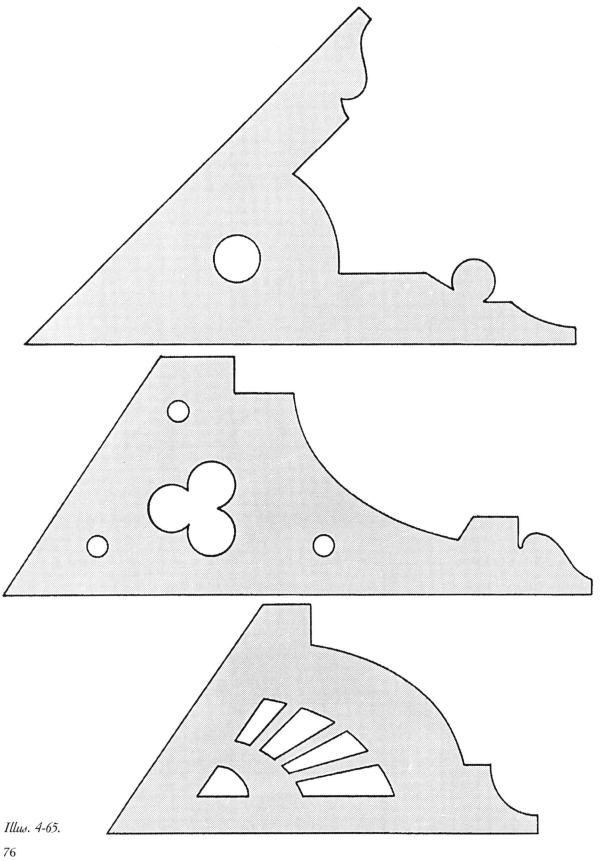

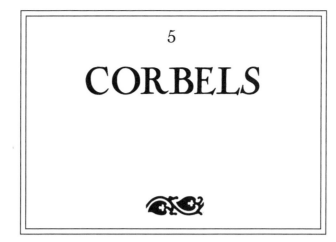

5

CORBELS

Corbels are very much like brackets, except that they are typically more massive-looking and much thicker than flat, sawn brackets. Corbels were often used to give physical support to a building projection. When they did not actually provide structural strength, their massive size gave support visually to the design of overhangs and under beams.

Today, old, salvaged corbels are much in demand for interior-decorating schemes. They are used to support mantels and are hung on the wall to support plants, statues, and other decorations.

Corbels are often made of several layers of thinner woods put together. Sometimes thick layers are combined with thinner, decorative or scroll-cut layers applied to the outer surfaces. See Illus. 5-1 through 5-4. As a rule, a corbel is seldom less than 1½ inch in thickness. Usually they are considerably heavier, up to 6 or 8 inches in overall thickness.

Illus. 5-1. A basic corbel. This style consists of thinner prepierced outside layers glued to a thicker inside layer of the same size and shape.

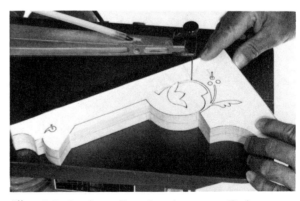

Illus. 5-2. Stack-scroll-sawing the two outside layers.

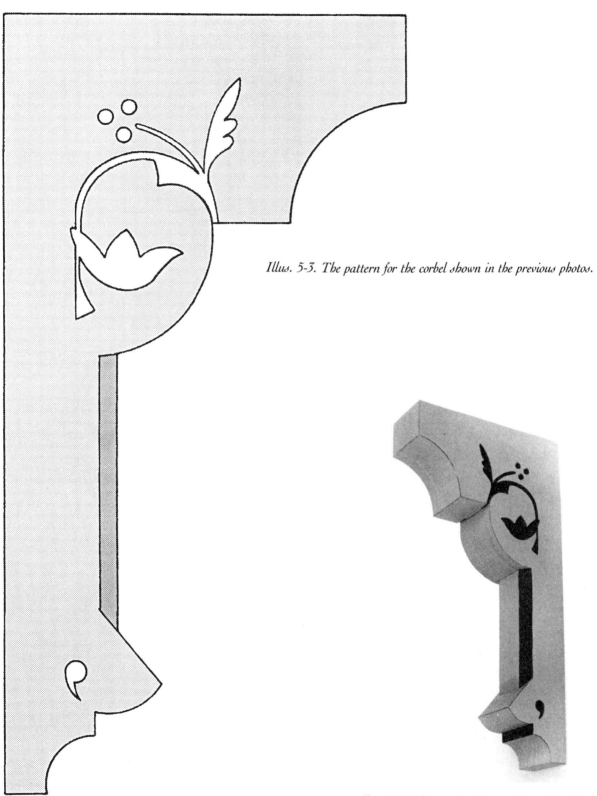

Illus. 5-3. The pattern for the corbel shown in the previous photos.

Illus. 5-4. The completed, painted corbel, with a stopped bevel at the side edges.

Interior layers of some corbel designs are often sawn to profiles that are shaped or cut differently from the outside layers. These corbels have an added dimension to their visual appeal.

Corbels can also be made of a single thickness of wood. See Illus. 5-5 and 5-6. Like brackets, corbels can be made to appear more massive by adding side frame boards to them, as shown in Illus. 5-8.

Making corbels is fun for the all-around woodworker because so many techniques can be incorporated. Adding turned finials or drops give corbels visual appeal. See Illus. 5-7 and 5-9. Non-turners can purchase ready-made turnings and attach them to their corbels.

Add extra mouldings around the tops, or groove flutes along the forward edges. Add your own special features to make one-of-a-kind exclusive creations. Individualize corbels with creative painting and finishing.

Illus. 5-5. A simple corbel made from one thick piece of wood.

Illus. 5-6.

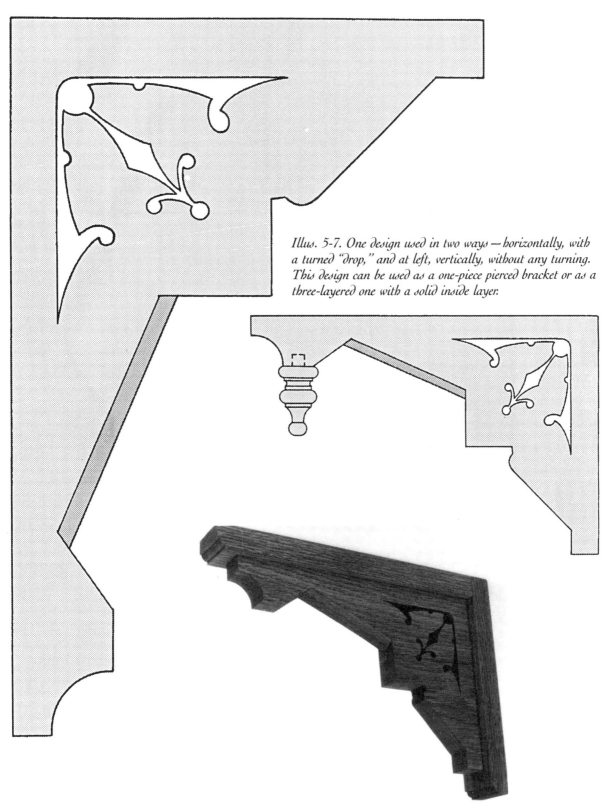

Illus. 5-7. One design used in two ways — horizontally, with a turned "drop," and at left, vertically, without any turning. This design can be used as a one-piece pierced bracket or as a three-layered one with a solid inside layer.

Illus. 5-8. A corbel with a side frame.

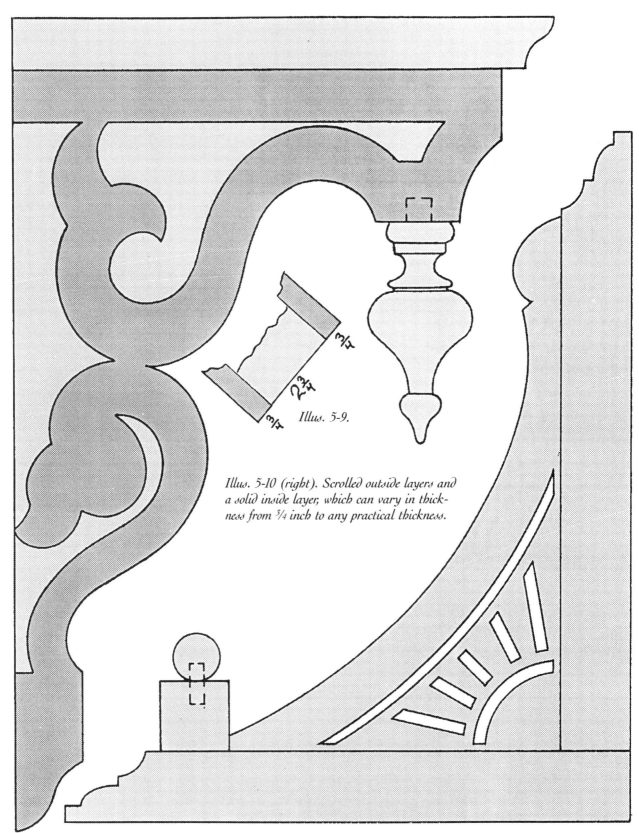

Illus. 5-9.

Illus. 5-10 (right). Scrolled outside layers and a solid inside layer, which can vary in thickness from ³⁄₄ inch to any practical thickness.

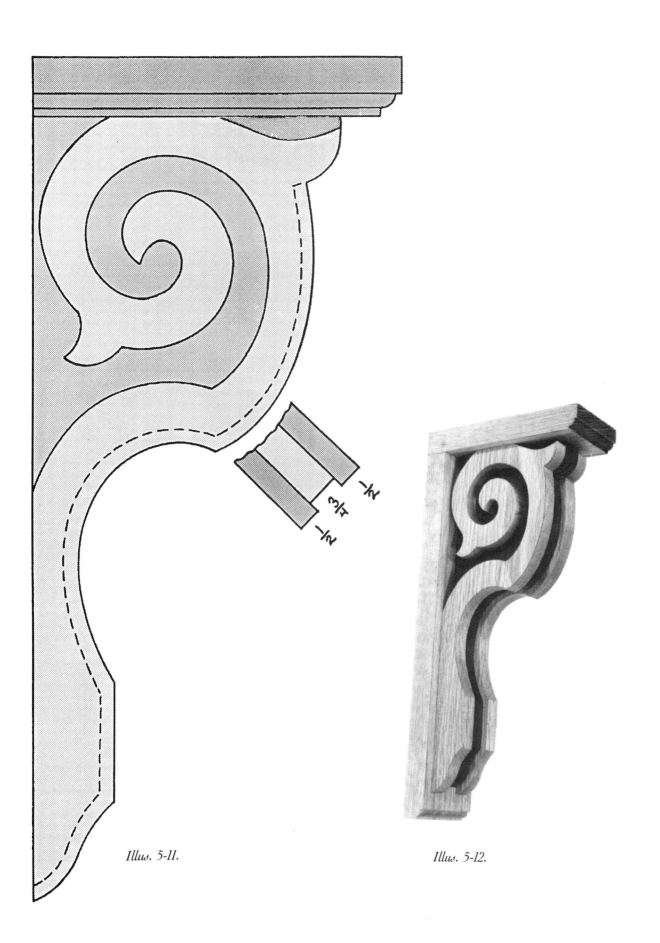

$\frac{1}{2}$

$\frac{3}{4}$

$\frac{1}{2}$

Illus. 5-11.

Illus. 5-12.

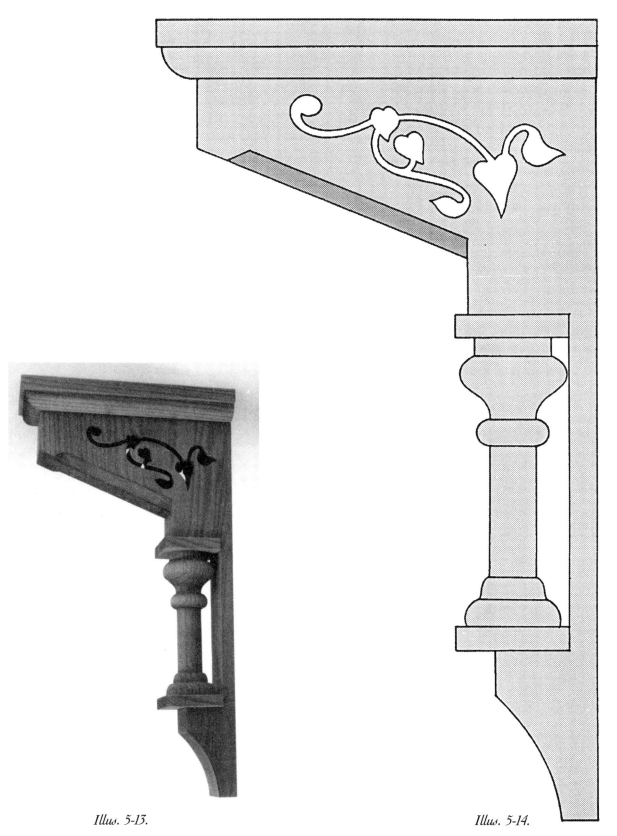

Illus. 5-13.

Illus. 5-14.

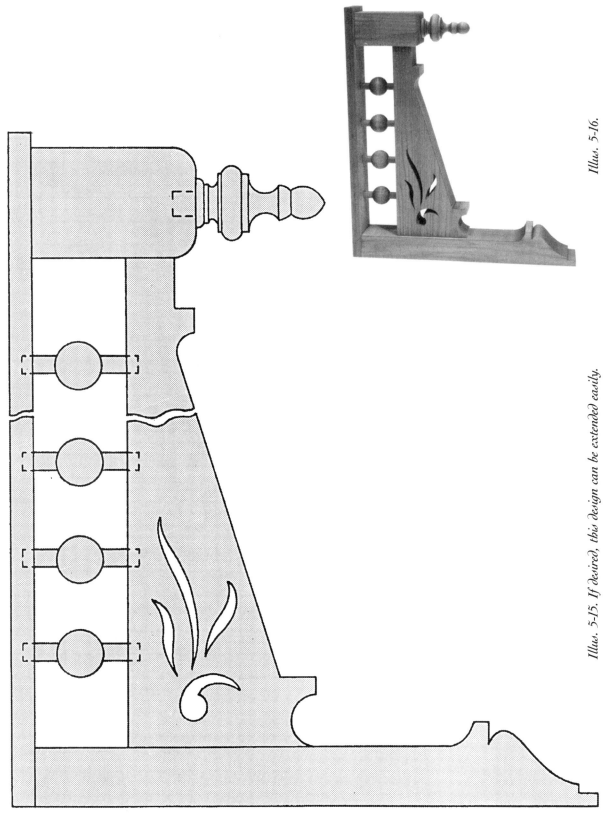

Illus. 5-15. If desired, this design can be extended easily.

Illus. 5-16.

84

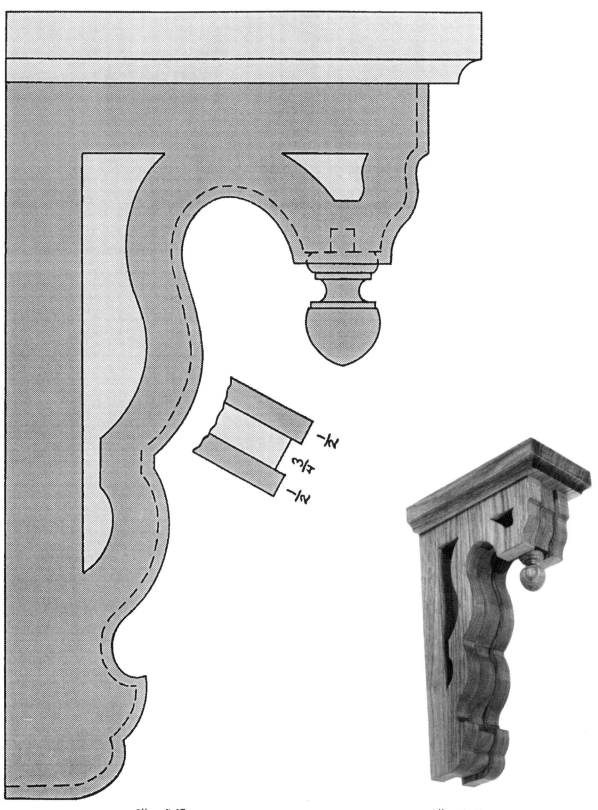

Illus. 5-17.

Illus. 5-18.

Illus. 5-19. A corbel with some distinctive but basic construction features. Note that the inside is a different profile shape from the outside layers. This project incorporates the use of mouldings and optional grooved flutes along the forward edge.

Illus. 5-20. Setup for grooving the forward edge. Note the test piece, above left, used to check the groove spacings.

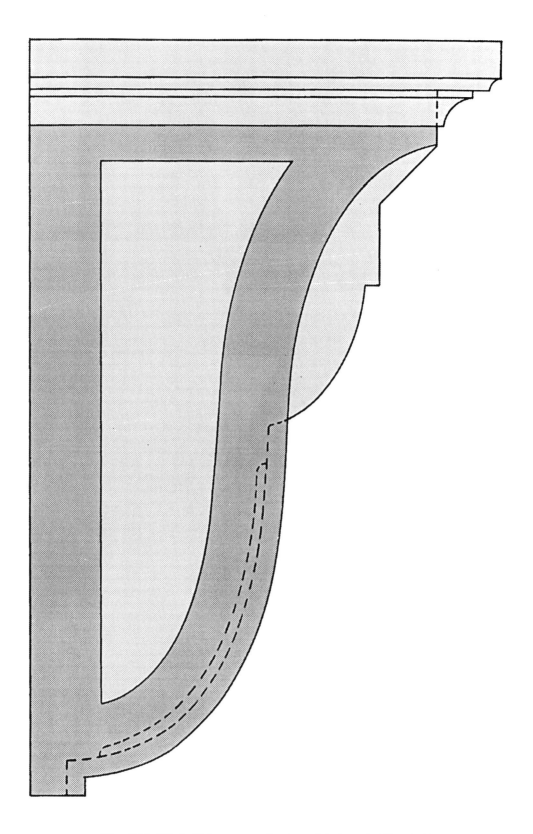

Illus. 5-21. The half-size pattern for the corbel shown in Illus. 5-19.

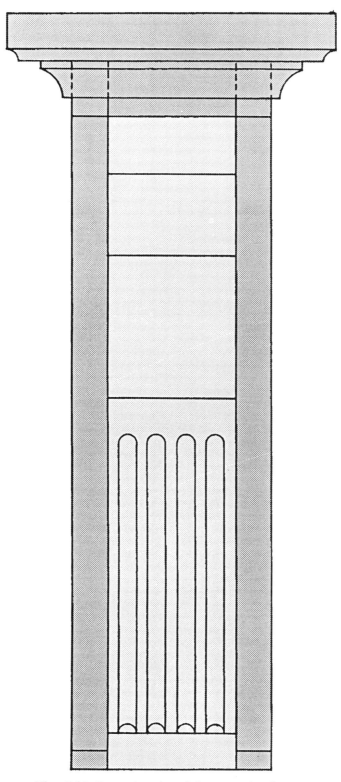

Illus. 5-22. Front-view plan of the pattern in Illus. 5-21.

Illus. 5-23 and Illus. 5-24. Two variations made from the same pattern (Illus. 5-25), each with an inside layer of a different thickness.

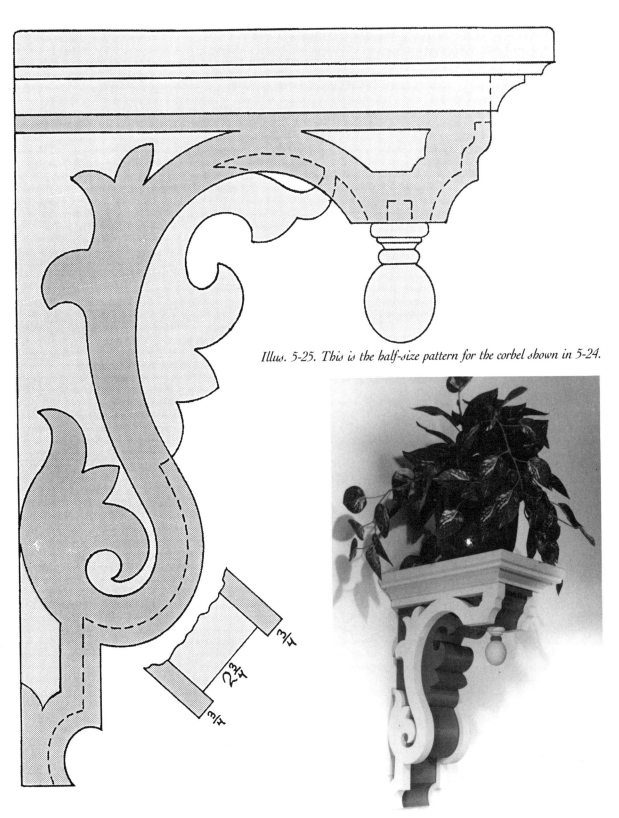

Illus. 5-25. This is the half-size pattern for the corbel shown in 5-24.

Illus. 5-26. Corbel pattern used as a shelf.

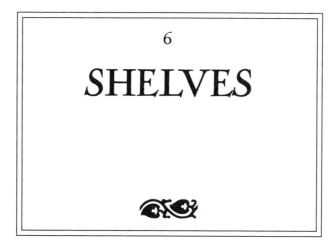

6

SHELVES

Flat sawn brackets, corbels, and even the fan brackets illustrated in the next chapter lend themselves well for use as shelves or shelf supports. With creative use of the patterns given on the previous pages you can make a wide variety of distinctive Victorian-styled shelving in any custom length and/or width desired.

Illus. 6-1 shows a simple shelf. This is just one example of many shelf possibilities made using flat, sawn brackets.

Shelf Hangers (Illus. 6-2). Many types of metal hangers and interlocking connectors are available for hanging either small, light shelves or massive corbels. One of the simplest types is a flat, metal hanger. It is shown in Illus. 6-3 nailed to the shelf.

Shelf-mounting techniques that hide or conceal fasteners and hardware are somewhat more involved, but are well worth a little extra effort. Use a router to cut a

Illus. 6-1. This small shelf consists of a ³⁄₄ × 5¹⁄₂ × 18-inch shelf with brackets.

Illus. 6-2. A variety of hardware is available for hanging shelves.

Illus. 6-4. This style of shelf hanger is concealed. It hooks over a screw inserted into the wall.

Illus. 6-5. Router-table setup for cutting a recess for a concealed shelf hanger. The workpiece is guided against a fence to the point indicated by a pencil mark on the fence.

Illus. 6-3. A simple shelf hanger fastened to the shelf.

Illus. 6-6. Larger shelf components can be mounted to walls with these concealed interlocking clips. The clip on the shelf or corbel meshes into a matching clip attached to the wall.

recess into the rear edge of the bracket or corbel, as shown in Illus. 6-4 to 6-6. This type of work is best done with the help of a router table and a guiding fence clamped to it to control the cut. See Illus. 6-5.

Illus. 6-6 shows a heavy-duty interlocking hanger system recommended for large, thick projects such as for corbel-styled shelving. The two corbel designs shown in Illus. 5-26 and 6-11 when used as shelves are wall-mounted with concealed interlocking hangers. The hangers are available from the Woodworker's Store, Rogers, Minnesota, and other mail-order sources.

Illus. 6-9. This pair of teardrop brackets makes some very interesting shelves. See page 71 for the full-size pattern. These accompany the shelves in Illus. 6-8 and 6-9.

Illus. 6-7 and Illus. 6-8. Ornamentation is added to the shelf piece itself with ball-and-dowel construction. This shelf measures ¾ × 6½ × 18¼ inches. The dowel holes are drilled 1⅝ inches on center along the edges.

Illus. 6-10. An interior corbel is both functional and ornamental in a Victorian decorating plan.

7

FAN BRACKETS

Unlike sawn brackets or corbels, fan brackets consist of dowel-and-ball construction or of spindles that jet outward from the inside corner. Fan brackets, which usually produce a delicate look, can be used interchangeably with other brackets. They are frequently used in conjunction with spandrels inside homes or on home exteriors. See Illus. 7-1.

Fan brackets are of two basic types: the ball-and-dowel-construction type (Illus. 7-2 and 7-3) and the turned-spindle type. Most manufactured balls are 1 inch in diameter and have predrilled holes for ⅜-inch-diameter dowel stock. These are the most popular sizes, but other sizes are available and the accompanying patterns may be scaled either up or down. Pre-turned spindles in various designs, shapes and lengths are also available.

No one style of ball or spindle construction is more popular or original than any other, so choose only those that appeal to you. The only difficulty in making fancy fan brackets is finding a good, simple technique for drilling the dowel or spindle holes into the matching pieces at the correct angles. This problem can be solved by making two basic jigs: (1) a layout board and (2) a drilling guide.

The Layout Board (Illus. 7-4) is simply a piece of plywood with two thin strips nailed onto it, forming a 90-degree inside corner. The circular segments are simply positioned properly and held in place as their holes are marked. See Illus. 7-5 and 7-6. Prepare in advance a paper master pattern that is marked with the number of dowels or spindles required and their angle spacings. The angles are best determined as follows: First, select the number of dowels or spindles you wish to use. Divide that number by 90. The number that results will be the interior angle. Divide the interior

Illus. 7-1. Fan-spindle-type brackets anchor each end of the connecting spandrels on these porches.

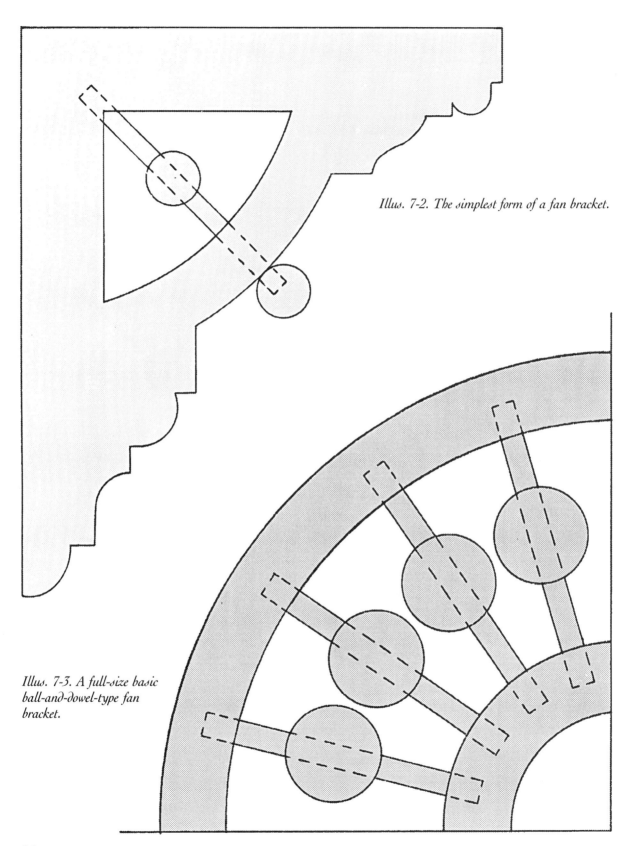

Illus. 7-2. The simplest form of a fan bracket.

Illus. 7-3. A full-size basic ball-and-dowel-type fan bracket.

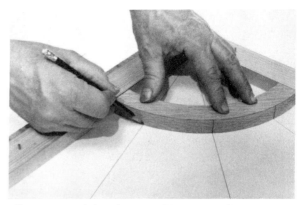

Illus. 7-4. This layout board measures 16 × 16 inches overall. Angular lines drawn on paper indicate the location of the centers of the dowels or spindles and their directions.

Illus. 7-5. Each dowel- or spindle-center line is transferred to each circular segment of the bracket.

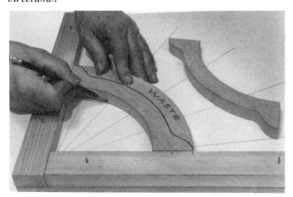

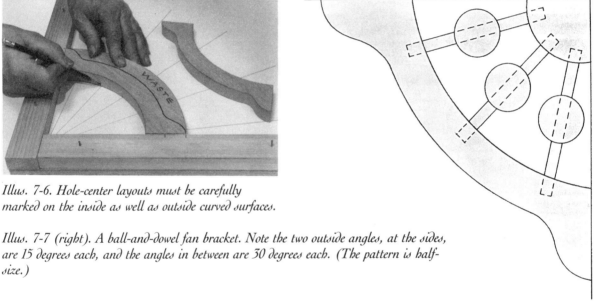

Illus. 7-6. Hole-center layouts must be carefully marked on the inside as well as outside curved surfaces.

Illus. 7-7 (right). A ball-and-dowel fan bracket. Note the two outside angles, at the sides, are 15 degrees each, and the angles in between are 30 degrees each. (The pattern is half-size.)

angle by 2 to find the two outside angles. For example, if your bracket will have three dowels (Illus. 7-7) or spindles, the first outside angles would be 15 degrees each and the two interior angles would be 30 degrees each.

The Drilling Guide (Illus. 7-8) is used to center-drill the dowel or spindle holes in the concave or convex edges of the curved bracket segments. To make this jig, start with a piece of plywood ¾ × 17 × 14 inches, which will become the base. Other interchangeable pieces will be made and attached to this base. One important part is the drill-guide piece itself, which consistently controls and guides the direction of the bit. This part (Illus. 7-9) is attached with screws to the base. Its center is aligned with a primary center line, which is marked on the base piece. The drill-guide blocks are

Illus. 7-8. The baseboard for the drilling guide and a pivoting block are used to drill corner pieces, like the one shown at the left.

Illus. 7-9. A close-up look at the interchangeable drill-guide blocks. Note their center lines and the optional bronze bushings, which should be used for production work. These are hardwood blocks ¾ × 1 × 3 inches in size.

carefully predrilled to accommodate metal bushings if desired. Metal bushings in ¼-, ⅜-, and ½-inch inside-diameter sizes can be found at good hardware stores or industrial-farm supply centers. It is not essential to use drill bushings unless you intend to make fan brackets in quantity. However, you do need a good, accurate hole in the drill block to guide the bit. Incidentally, an opening cut through the base just behind the drill-guide block permits shavings to fall through.

A pivoting block (Illus. 7-8 and 7-10) fits into a hole located along the primary center line of the base. The exact location of the ½-inch-diameter pivoting hole will depend upon the size of the corner blocks that are to be drilled. The part to be drilled should be fairly close to the drill-bit guide block. This block consists of a ½-inch-diameter dowel and a ¾ × 3 × 4-inch block. Make this with a right-angle opening cut so its apex is at the exact center of the vertical dowel, shown in Illus. 7-8. This block is used only when drilling the "radiused" corner blocks.

Illus. 7-11 and 7-12 show how the circular segments are drilled into their convex and concave edges, respectively. Special work-holding panels are sawn from ¾-inch plywood to match the inside and outside curves of the circular segments that need drilling. These are nailed (or screwed) to the base with their center lines aligned over the primary center line (drilling direction) of the base. *Note:* When center-drilling into stock pieces that are greater than ¾ inch in thickness, shim under the drilling-guide block as necessary. When drilling into segments that are less than ¾ inch thick, shim under the pieces actually being drilled. Screen-door fan brackets, for example, are usually just ½ inch thick.

If you plan to produce identical parts in two or more separate work sessions,

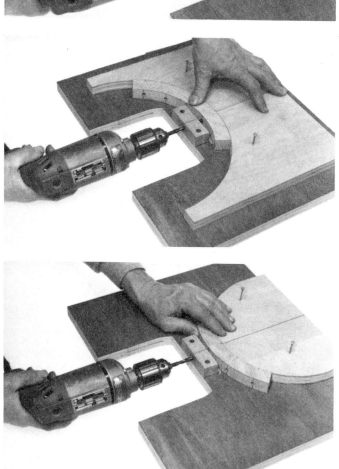

Illus. 7-10. Drilling a corner block.

Illus. 7-11. Drilling holes into the inside edge of a curved fan-bracket segment.

Illus. 7-12. Drilling into the outside edge of a curved segment.

arrange various stops. That way, you can avoid marking the centers for each hole. Use spur-point-type bits to drill cleaner, sharp holes at any angle to the grain direction. *Assembly tips:* Wood balls can either be glued or nailed to the dowels in their proper locations. Glue in all spindle and dowel ends. Finally, be sure that all parts are assembled in a flat plane. Careless assembly will result in a distorted or twisted bracket.

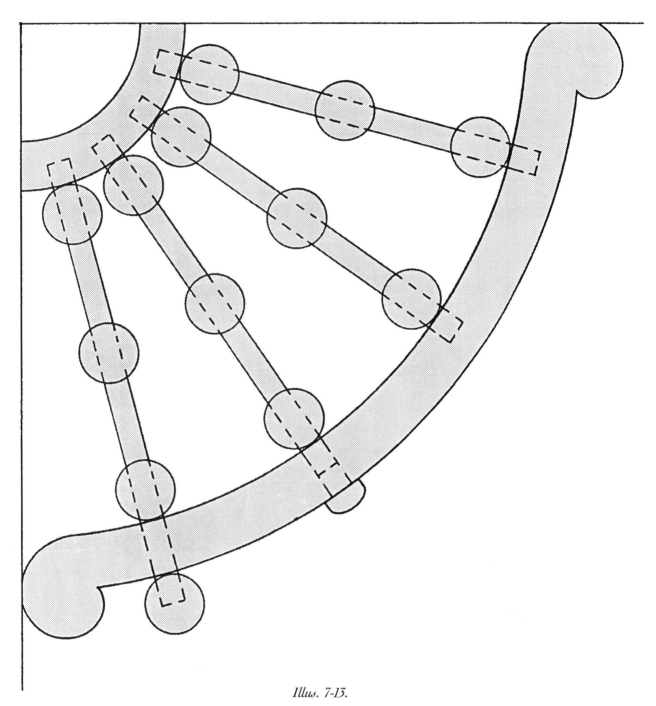

Illus. 7-13.

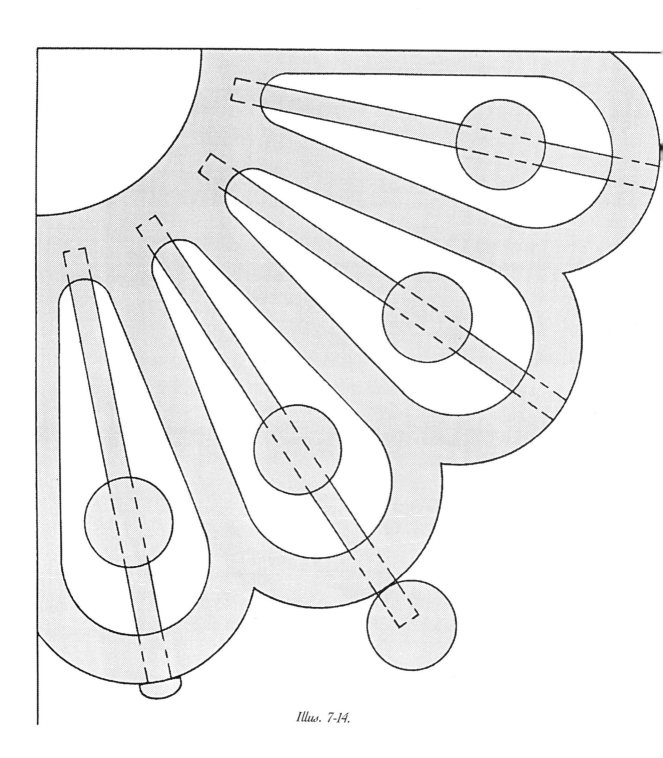

Illus. 7-14.

Илл. 7-15.

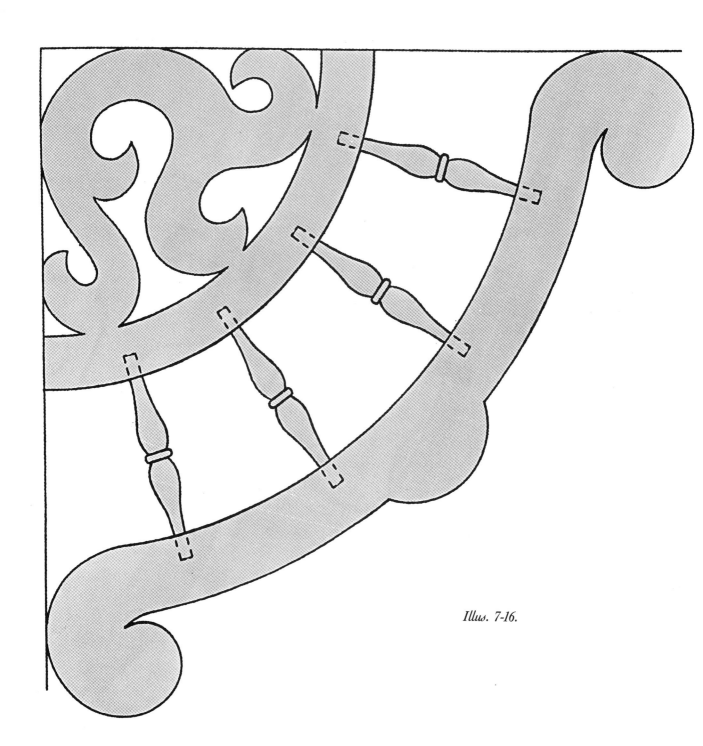

Illus. 7-16.

8

GRILLES AND SPANDRELS

Grilles and spandrels, like fan brackets, are made of ball-and-dowel or turned-spindle construction. These are usually framed sections that are used to span various openings.

Making authentic reproductions of the beautiful old grilles and spandrels, shown in Illus. 8-1 and 8-2, is one of the ultimate challenges for the amateur woodworker. This chapter presents ideas on how to make basic grilles and spandrels. The reproductions of old, authentic interior grillework are included to spark your interest and imagination.

Grilles and spandrels traditionally were made of oak, birch, or yellow pine. Today, most millwork companies producing interior gingerbread grilles and spandrels use poplar, clear pine, or clear-heart redwood. The dowels and turnings are birch, maple, or oak.

Spandrels can be used to span various openings inside and outside the home. Chapter 9 demonstrates how various spandrel designs are used on porches or patios, from post to post, under overhangs, roofs and entrances. There are many creative indoor uses for custom-made spandrels and grilles. Use them between kitchen cabinets, over the sink or home bar, or in the bathroom. Hang a narrow spandrel from the ceiling to set off a special area within a large room, such as over a hot tub, library, or exercise area.

When designing spandrels and grilles for a specific application, be sure to allow for sufficient head-room clearances. Also, consider including decorative fan brackets to give visual support at the ends of the spandrel runs. See Illus. 8-3 and 8-4. Most ball-and-dowel spandrels are made from 1-inch-diameter wood balls on ⅜-inch dowels.

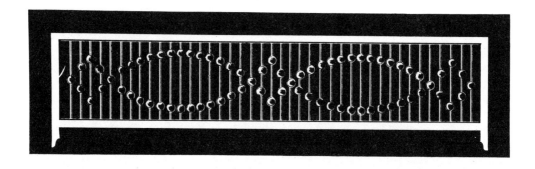

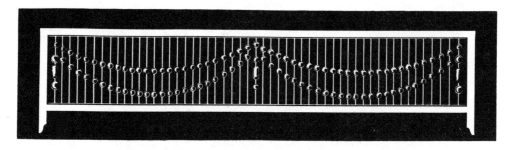

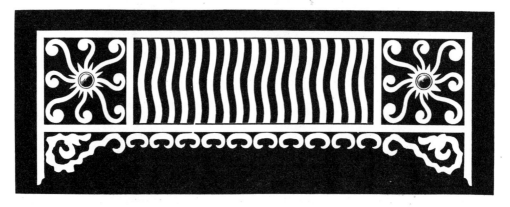

*Illus. 8-1. This artwork, reproduced from early catalogs, shows some relatively uncompli-
cated spandrels and brackets. Below, an exterior porch grille made of all sawn parts. Note
the two examples of fancy fan brackets. These were typically used with spandrels to achieve
elaborate interior gingerbread ornamentation.*

Illus. 8-2. More authentic Victorian-era spandrel and grille designs featuring scrollwork with ball-and-dowel construction.

Illus. 8-3. This basic ball-and-dowel spandrel was made with the holes 1½ inch on centers drilled into oak framing ¾ × 2 inches wide.

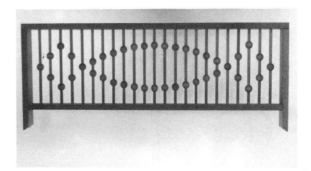

Illus. 8-4. Essentially the same construction but with fan brackets added.

Begin with a paper layout drawn to scale, or draw a full-size chalk plan of your layout on cardboard or on the shop floor. Typical dowel spacings are 1½ inches on center. The horizontal rails or frame stock are usually ¾ inches thick and 1½ to 2 inches wide.

The sample spandrels we've made are shown in Illus. 8-3 and 8-4. One of the tricks to drilling the dowel-spacing holes in the frame rails is shown in Illus. 8-5. This simple setup automatically positions the workpiece so all the holes are drilled to uniform center-to-center spacings without measuring or marking.

Clamp a straight-edge fence to the drill-press table. To this fence attach a block with a vertically removable dowel. Locate the dowel away from the bit at a distance equal to the center-to-center spacing desired. After the first hole is drilled in the workpiece (and for each successive hole thereafter) shift the piece along the fence until the dowel slips into the previously drilled hole. This automatically positions the piece for drilling the next hole. Illus. 8-6 shows one method of drilling holes at right angles to each other. This setup can be used to make the kind of ornate grille-work where dowels appear to intersect each other through the wood balls at 90-degree angles.

Illus. 8-5. The setup for drilling equally spaced holes in the rail framings. As each hole is drilled, the workpiece is shifted to the right to a point where the dowel drops into the previously drilled hole, automatically positioning the workpiece for the next hole to be drilled.

Illus. 8-6. Some very fancy grille and spandrel work has dowels intersecting through the balls at 90 degrees, as shown at the upper right. This setup, using a "V"-block and a scrap length of dowel, makes perfectly centered, perpendicular holes.

PORCH SPANDRELS

Our preference in home design is for the charm and function of a porch. See Illus. 9-1 and 9-2. Today, old-style reproduction porches, sheltered decks and patios are being decorated with spandrels extending from post to post or wall to post for some dramatic entrances.

The variety of designs offer an array of choices from simple square spindles (Illus. 9-4) to ornate turned ones (Illus. 9-3) to typical ball-and-dowel construction, as shown in Illus. 9-5. Light to heavier spandrel turnings can be purchased ready-turned from building supply centers, or you can spin out your own with a lathe if you are so inclined.

Illus. 9-6 and 9-7 show some simple ideas for spandrels you can create using

Illus. 9-1. An authentic Victorian porch incorporating beautiful spindle-type spandrels with decorative turnings and ornate brackets.

Illus. 9-2. Narrow, thin spandrels and delicate fan brackets are visual attractions that frame the front entrance to this Victorian-style home.

Illus. 9-3. Typical porch detailing of the Victorian period. Note the pierced panel and the brackets used with the turned spindles in this spandrel construction.

purchased spindles with pierced panels and flat sawn brackets cut with a scroll saw. Fan brackets highlight the spandrels dramatically. They are complementary additions where space and visual compatibility permit their use. See Illus. 9-8.

The previous chapter offers some helpful tips pertaining to drilling equally spaced holes in the spandrel railings. Square spindles or turned ones with squared ends can be nailed or doweled in place.

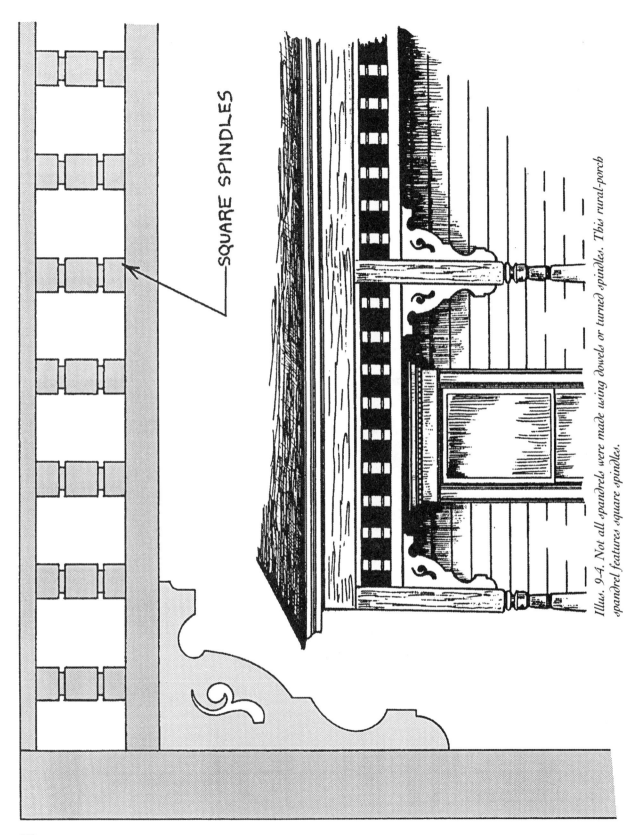

SQUARE SPINDLES

Illus. 9-4. Not all spandrels were made using dowels or turned spindles. This rural-porch spandrel features square spindles.

Illus. 9-5. Basic ball-and-dowel spandrel design with pierced-panel detail.

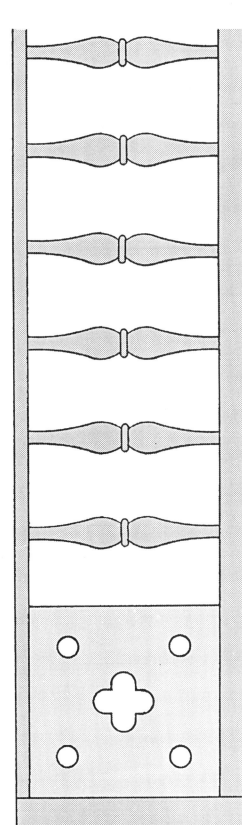

Illus. 9-6 and Illus. 9-7.

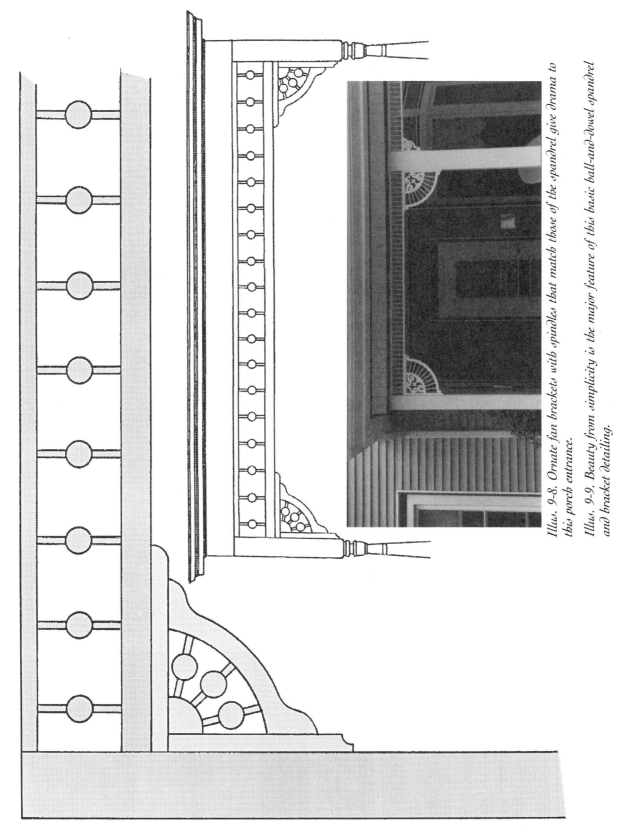

Illus. 9-8. Ornate fan brackets with spindles that match those of the spandrel give drama to this porch entrance.

Illus. 9-9. Beauty from simplicity is the major feature of this basic ball-and-dowel spandrel and bracket detailing.

113

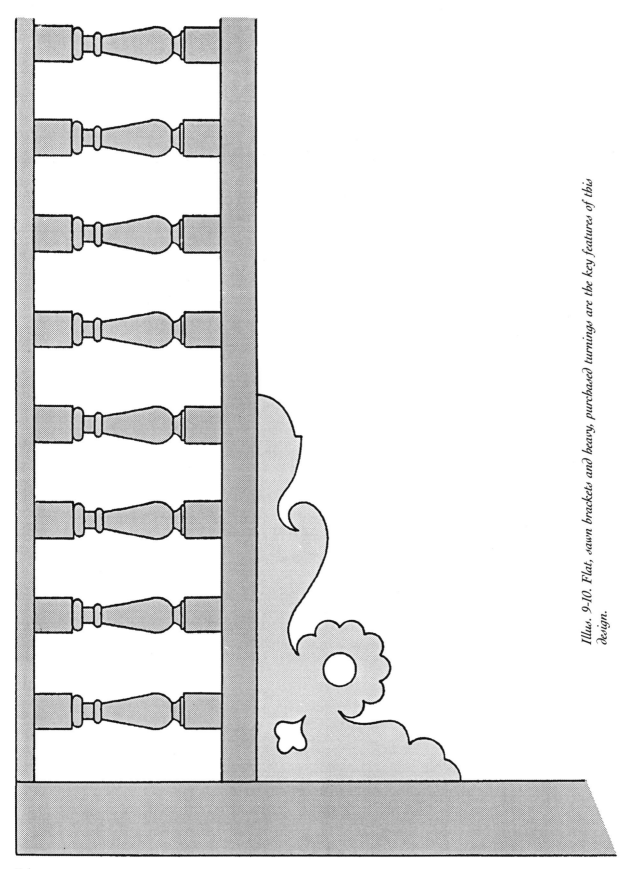

Illus. 9-10. Flat, sawn brackets and heavy, purchased turnings are the key features of this design.

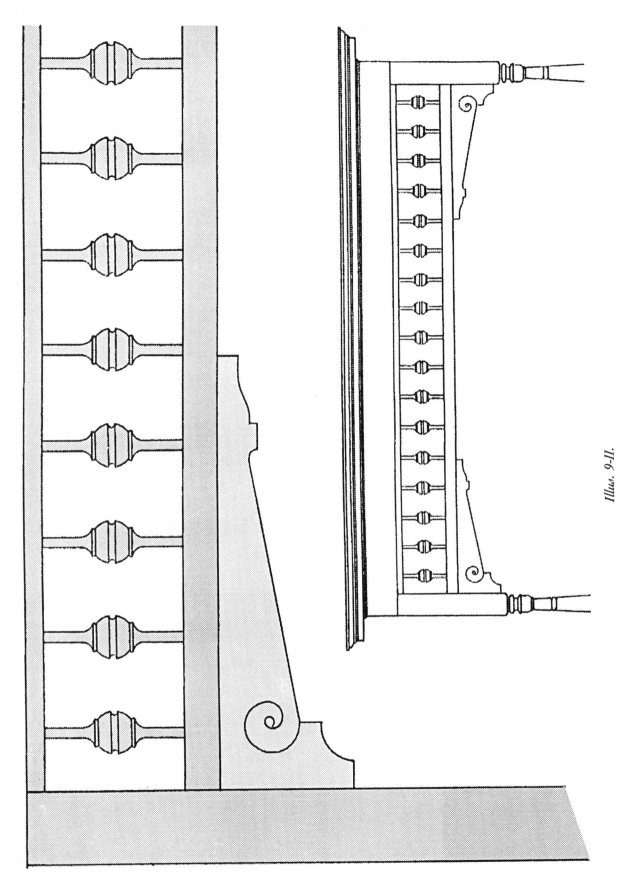

115

10

SAWN BALUSTERS

All elevated porches and decks need some type of protective railing. The easiest and often the most appropriate design incorporates decorative sawn balusters. See Illus. 10-1.

Sawn balusters are easy to make. A number of the most popular designs appear in this chapter. They are on gridded patterns and must be enlarged. They are actually half patterns — in other words, they must be flipped on their vertical centers to create the full-pattern width. Draw your grid in 1-inch squares and copy the design square by square.

The standard heights (lengths) of balusters vary. The standard sizes are: 23, 24, and 27 inches. The patterns here are scaled to 24 inches. Simply add 1½ inches to each end to make the longer, 27-inch size, or cut ½ inch off each end to make the popular 23-inch sizes.

Illus. 10-1. Porch designs incorporating posts, brackets, and running trim with sawn and turned balusters attached to railing stock. (Photo courtesy of Silverton Victorian Millworks).

Sawn balusters are best cut from redwood or cedar. Cedar is the most practical choice. Commercially made balusters may be cut from poplar or pine. Usually it's easiest to cut one and use it as a template or master pattern for the others. Saw with a band saw or hand-held electric scroll/jig saw. Designs that have true circular segments or true round holes are best made on a drill press or bored by hand. See Illus. 10-2. Often, half-circle cuts butt up against one another, making a continuing pattern along the full distance of the installation.

Illus. 10-2. Drill-press set up for boring a circular segment of the profile. Here a fence and stop block are used to assure that every hole will be made in every baluster in exactly the same location. The workpiece is flipped over to make the second hole with the same end held against the stop.

Once all balusters are cut out, they need to be attached to a top handrail and a bottom, or lower, rail. There are many ways to do this. The better methods provide for good drainage. Illus. 10-3 shows many different ways to make this assembly. Most assembly systems revolve around some form of lengthwise groove, rabbet, or "L"-shaped groove that can be cut with a router or on the table saw.

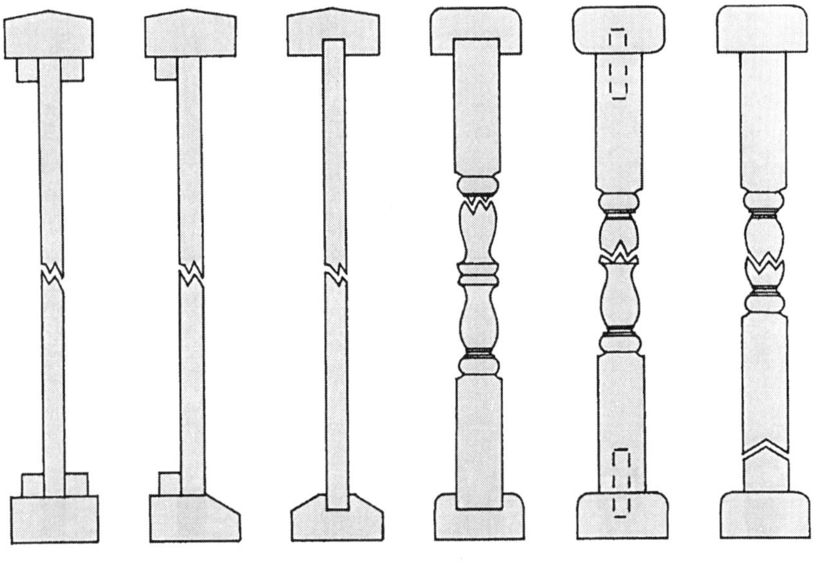

Illus. 10-3. Cross sections showing different ways to assemble sawn and turned balusters to the top handrail and bottom rail.

It is a good idea to coat all parts with a penetrating preservative and/or a water repellant and to allow them to dry before painting and assembly. It may be more practical to make all the balusters into rail assemblies and then set the entire rail assembly into place. For the strongest construction, set the ends of the rails into routed or chiseled recesses cut into the sides of the posts. An alternate technique is to use metal, right-angle bracket-type connectors screwed underneath the ends of the top rail and into the sides of posts or into a stud on an abutting wall. Another method is to fasten a cleat between the top and bottom rails on each end of the rail assembly. Fasten this cleat to the post or abutting wall.

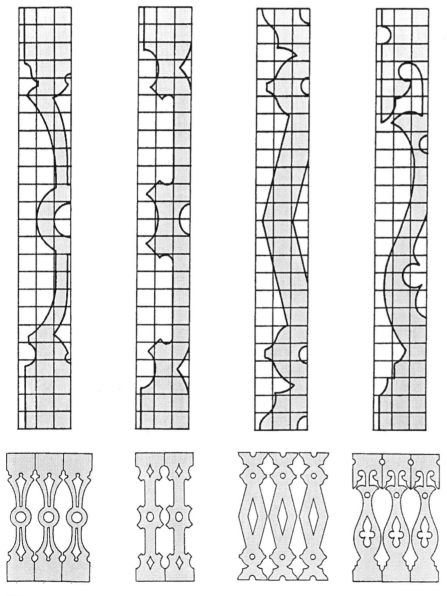

Illus. 10-4.

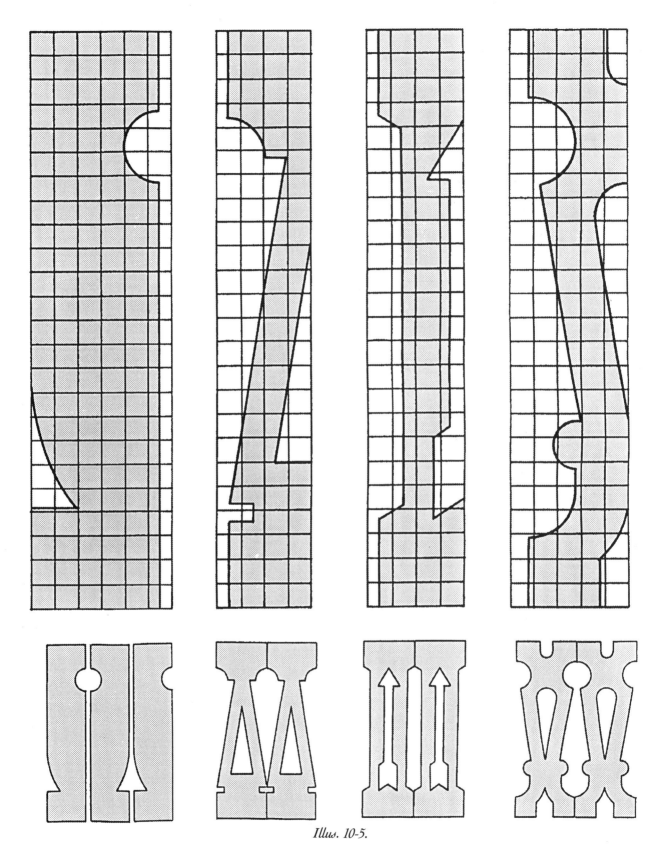

Illus. 10-5.

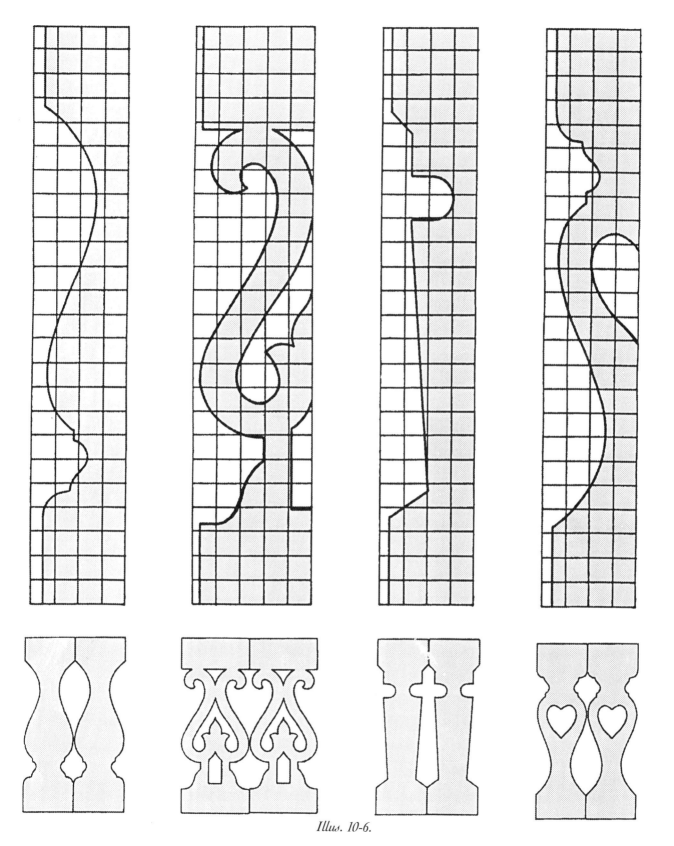

Illus. 10-6.

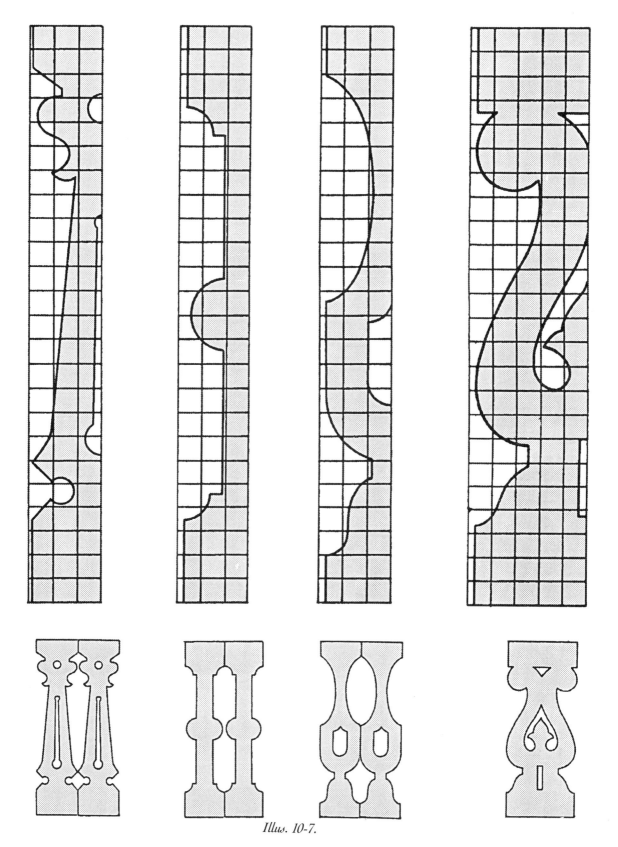

Illus. 10-7.

RUNNING TRIM

Using a repeating design sawn into a continuous length of narrow wood can give an otherwise-drab look a very spicy lift. Similarly, using running trim in Victorian gingerbread installations (Illus. 11-1) offers visual interest and gives continuity to the overall design plan. Various repeating designs were widely used on Victorian homes to give a lacy or frilly look to the bottom edges of the fascia board that runs along the roof line. Running trim is also widely used between porch posts where head-room space prohibits the use of spandrels. See Illus. 10-1 on page 116. Our Victorian rural mailboxes in Chapter 17 even have running trim attached to their mounting boards.

Running trim also has a number of good uses indoors, where spandrels may not allow sufficient head room. Shelf edges, doorways, arches, and almost any opening can be spanned with a length of running trim. There are many designs for running trim. We've included a few new ones here (Illus. 11-2) with full-size patterns

Illus. 11-1. This gable-end porch is decorated with a simple running design and a flat, sawn bracket.

following. These can be adjusted sizewise, if necessary. More running trim designs and patterns are given in Chapter 17. Although they are sized to decorate the rural mailbox mounting boards, the basic designs can be used anywhere. You can also find many other designs for running trim (brackets, etc.) in our book *Scroll Saw Fretwork Patterns* (Sterling, 1989).

Illus. 11-2. An array of running-trim patterns that follow in this chapter.

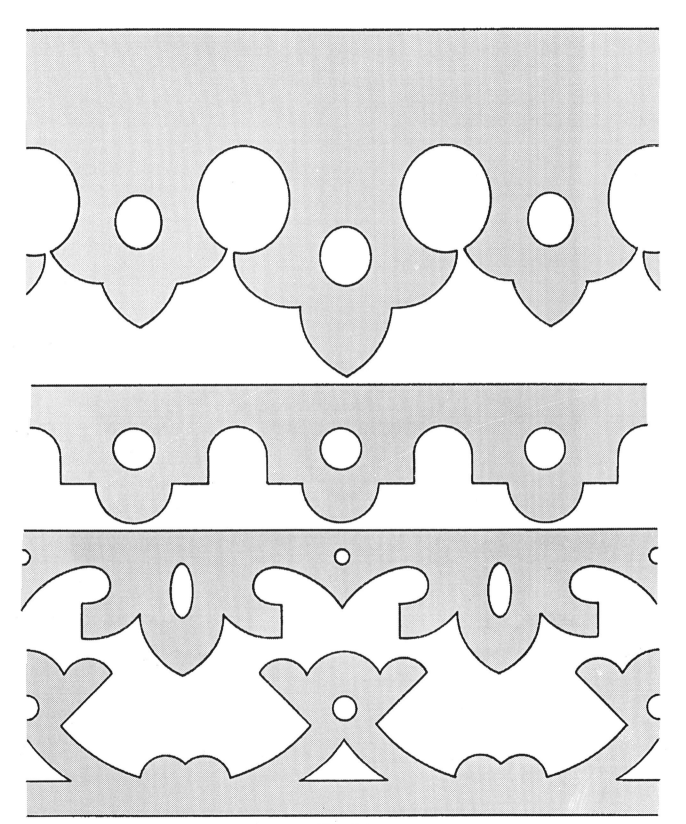

Illus. 11-3.

Illus. 11-4.

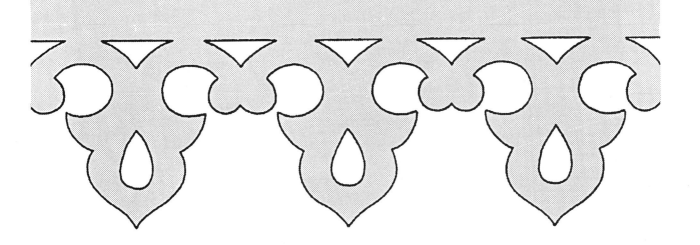

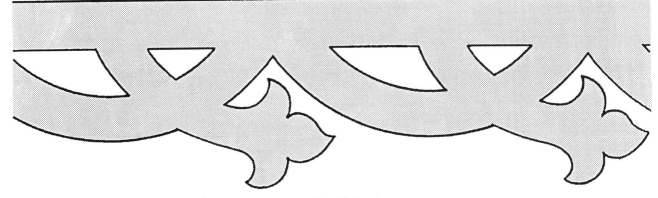

Illus. 11-5.

12

HEADERS

Headers are cutouts that are often used as overlays to decorate above doorways, windows (Illus. 12-1 and Illus. 12-5) and on gabled-end walls. Some headers can also be mounted inverted to hang from under shelves and along the bottom rails of porch or interior spandrels. Usually, headers are placed atop an assembly or on top of window and door casings indoors or out. Headers also decorate the top and bottom edges of hanging sign blanks and rural mailboxes with narrower designs. See Illus. 12-2 and 12-3.

Some of these half patterns may be appropriate to use in the size given in this book. Illus. 12-2 and 12-3, intended for use on mailboxes, need to be enlarged 125% to more than double the size they appear here.

When used as overlays, headers are usually painted or finished before installation, unless their finish will be the same as the material the header will be applied to.

Illus. 12-1. Headers are widely used over windows, doors, and against gable-end walls.

Illus. 12-2. These narrow headers are also used for decorating the rural mailboxes described in Chapter 17.

128

Illus. 12-3.

Illus. 12-4. More header designs used for mailbox ornamentation. Note how the upper-half pattern was converted to a bracket, as shown by the insert photo, Illus. 12-3.

Илл. 12-5.

130

Illus. 12-6.

Illus. 12-7.

Illus. 12-8.

Illus. 12-9.

Illus. 12-10.

Илл. 12-11.

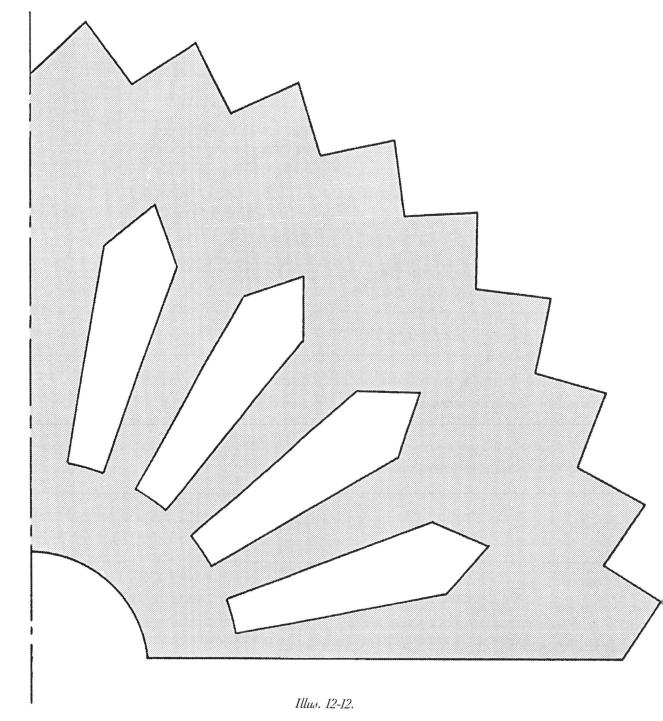

Illus. 12-12.

Valances are short, decorative cutouts designed to span windows. Valances can also be used as trim around built-in bookcases, entertainment centers, and other openings that are relatively narrow. Valances are used for much the same purpose as spandrels and running trim, but their use produces a somewhat different look. Sometimes, with height permitting, valances can actually be used with spandrels to span the very same openings. They can be placed below spandrel runs or even designed to terminate the endings of them.

If your opening size is already established, simply enlarge your choice of the given patterns to fit. The patterns can be extended horizontally by modifying the central area of the pattern or by inserting filler pieces designed to complement the overall design. Many of the valances included here have a somewhat repeating design element that can be extracted and added to the central area of the pattern to extend the horizontal dimension.

Illus. 13-1.

Illus. 13-2.

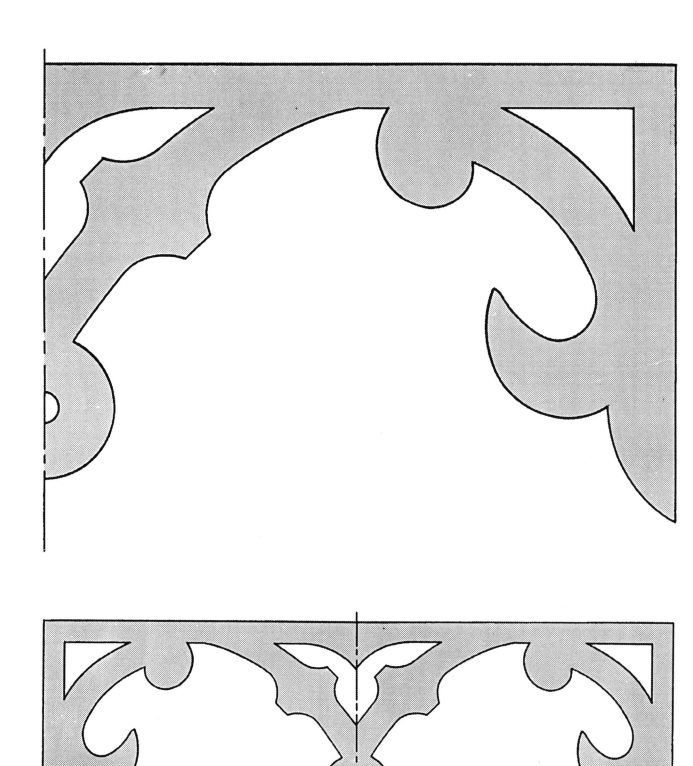

Illus. 13-3.

Illus. 13-4.

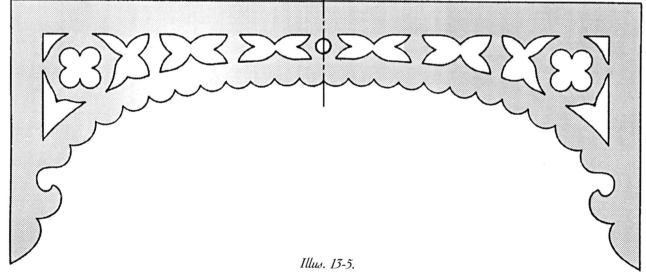

Illus. 13-5.

Illus. 13-6.

Illus. 13-7.

Illus. 13-8.

14

GABLE ORNAMENTS

Making and installing very ornate Victorian-style gable ornamentation (Illus. 14-1) is something best reserved for the more experienced carpenter. However, this chapter presents some basic patterns of gable ornaments that are relatively easy to make and install. The pattern design and the installation must be made to match the pitch, or included angles, created by the sloping roofs. The roof pitch is the amount a roof inclines vertically along one foot of distance horizontally. A 6/12 pitch means that the roof inclines 6 inches for every foot measured horizontally. Roofs generally vary from 4/12 to 12/12 pitches.

Finding the Angle for Gable Trim (Illus. 14-2). This process is fairly easy. Follow these basic steps: (1) Measure 24 inches (with a tape or a rigid rule) from the peak (point A) downwards along the bottom edge of the fascia board and mark point B. (2) Do the same along the other side, measuring down 24 inches. Mark point C. (3) Measure horizontally from point B to point C. (4) Now, on cardboard or your shop floor, lay out a straight line the distance of B–C. (5) Swing two arcs of 24-inch radius with one center at point B and one at point C. Where these two arcs cross is point A, or an angle identical to that of the peak of your roof.

You have re-created the exact angle of your gable. Now you can plan or modify any gable trim ornamentation using this angle without climbing up and down the ladder to make trial fits and adjustments.

Some gable ornaments are easier to modify than others. One design that is very easy to modify is given in Illus. 14-3. Some gable ornaments almost self-adjust to any pitch. Two such patterns appear in Illus. 14-4 and 14-5. There is even an adjustable

Illus. 14-1. Beautiful gable ornamentation. (Design and fabrication by the Honey Tree Wood Shop.)

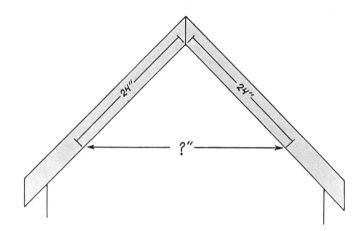

Illus. 14-2. Establishing the gable angle.

gable ornament. It consists of four individual pieces, shown in Illus. 14-7. Illus. 14-6 and 14-8 are the pattern pieces for this adjustable gable ornament.

Another style gable ornamentation that will fit almost any pitch is based on a design for running trim. One such pattern is given in Illus. 14-9. The upper ends of the running trim abut against a vertical center-post drop. The top of this post must be cut to match the roof angles. The pattern can end anywhere — or can be extended the entire length of the gable. If it is extended the entire gable length, the lower end of the pattern may require some modification.

The pattern in Illus. 14-10 is another continuous-trim style for gable ornamentation. With slight modification to the upper end of the side pieces, this pattern can also be used on almost any pitched roof.

Patterns in Illus. 14-11 and 14-12 are prepared specifically for older-style houses that have a 12/12 pitch. With some modification they may be made to conform to a 10/12 pitch, but not much less.

Illus. 14-3. This very simple gable-ornament design is easy to modify to fit many various-pitched roofs.

Illus. 14-4. This gable ornament will fit most roof angles with little modification. The end of the center-post drop must be cut to match the roof angles.

Illus. 14-5. This two-piece ornament will accommodate itself to fit most roof pitches. Simply install each half so it just touches the other as shown. (Design courtesy of Grant Lanceleve.)

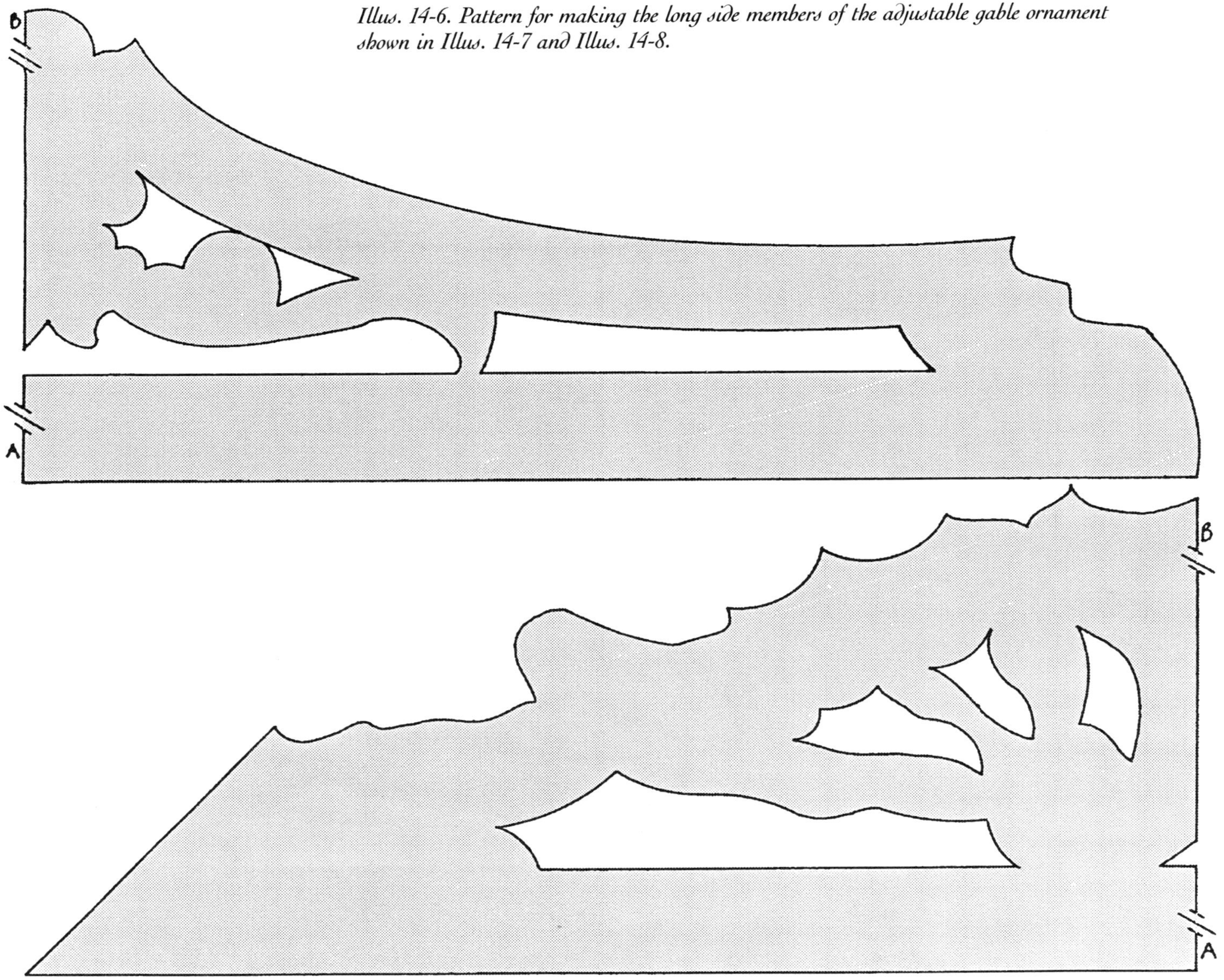

Illus. 14-6. Pattern for making the long side members of the adjustable gable ornament shown in Illus. 14-7 and Illus. 14-8.

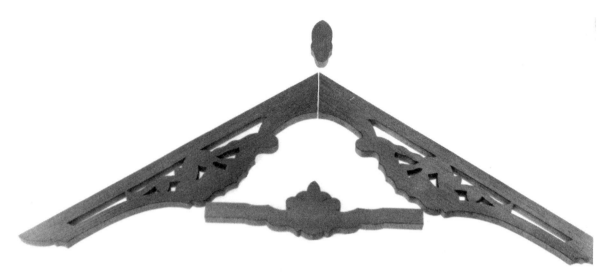

Illus. 14-7. Components for an adjustable gable ornament. The lower component, which is easily extended or shortened, fits behind the two side pieces. A small medallion is glued over the vertical splice at the top or peak.

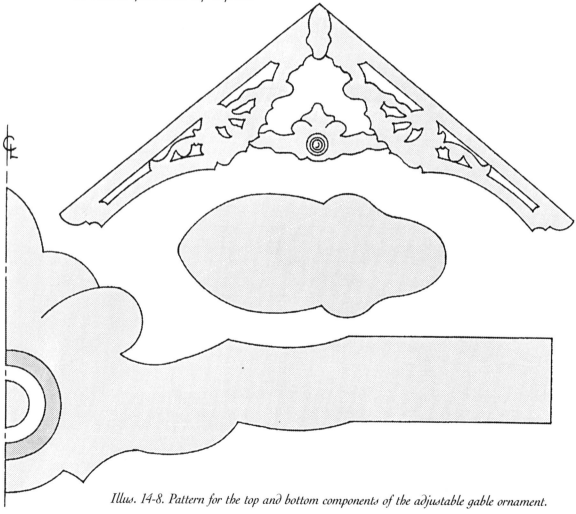

Illus. 14-8. Pattern for the top and bottom components of the adjustable gable ornament.

153

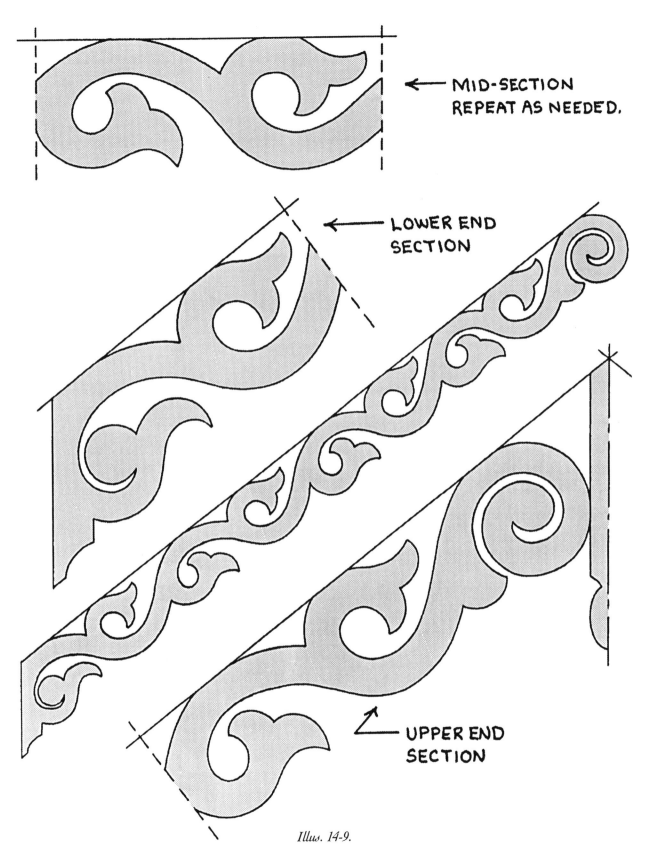

← MID-SECTION
REPEAT AS NEEDED.

← LOWER END
SECTION

UPPER END
SECTION

Illus. 14-9.

MID-SECTION
REPEAT AS NEEDED.

LOWER END
SECTION

UPPER END
SECTION

Illus. 14-10.

155

Illus. 14-11.

MID-SECTION
REPEAT AS NEEDED.

LOWER END
SECTION

UPPER END
SECTION

Illus. 14-12.

15

SCREEN DOORS

The front door of your home is an important visual focus. You can easily dress it up with brackets or other add-ons to give your guests a warm Victorian welcome. See Illus. 15-2.

Turn-of-the-century homes had beautiful screen doors (Illus. 15-1) to allow summer breezes and fresh air in and stale air out. In recent years, screen doors are making a very strong comeback despite modern air-conditioning.

Illus. 15-1. Some turn-of-the-century screen doors.

Illus. 15-2. This entrance designed and built by Grant Lanceleve gives a warm Victorian welcome. Note the screen door decorated with narrow spindle spandrels and corner brackets. See Illus. 4-20 for the door corner-bracket pattern.

buy one of the least expensive screen doors available and trim it yourself, attaching your own homemade brackets and spandrels. See Illus. 15-3. It is surprising how inexpensive this easy approach is, compared to purchasing a fully dressed Victorian-style one. Fancy Victorian-style screen doors can cost over ten times more than plain, unembellished ones.

A word of caution: Before making up any brackets — especially for a purchased screen door — be sure to check the overall thickness of the door. Also, check to see if the inside edges of the door framing are shaped or router-cut. The door may look best if you make all the brackets of thinner material than you would initially have planned to use. The fan bracket being installed, shown in Illus. 15-3, is only ½ inch in overall thickness. Anything thicker would protrude from the shaped edge of the door's frame. *Tip:* Always paint your door brackets and spandrels before fastening them into place.

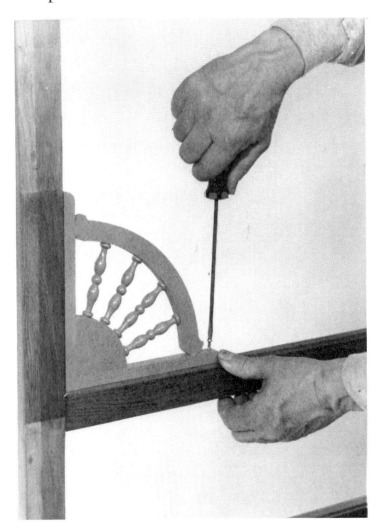

Illus. 15-3. An inexpensive screen door is easily dressed up simply by fastening brackets to the inside corners.

16
PICKET FENCES AND TRELLISES

The simple beauty of a Victorian cottage or home is enhanced considerably by picket fencing. Picket fences and trellises always add distinctive charm to a home. Illus. 16-1 gives various half-pattern designs in standard 36-inch lengths for some of the more ornately styled fences that were popular in the early 1900s.

To reproduce these designs full size, simply enlarge them with the grid system, transferring the design to the same number of 3-inch squares. Antique picket fences were usually a full 4 inches in width. You may want to alter your design slightly so it fits onto today's 1 × 4 stock, which is actually 3½ inches in width. This is easy to do. Illus. 16-2 gives some patterns for other popular picket-fence tops that can also be enlarged using the same 3-inch-square grid. Of course, they can be enlarged more easily on a copy machine, enlarging the original pattern five and one half times.

Trellis designs provide for the vertical growth of vines and flowers and accentuate areas of your home. Trellises can be a constant source of pleasure. They give nature an opportunity to display her charms and enrich the exterior atmosphere of your home. Judiciously placed against certain walls or a chimney, they create proper exterior balance and can break up barren-looking places. Often, trellises are built to be freestanding along a walk or driveway or at the edge of the lawn. When used freestanding, however, they should be constructed from heavier material.

Use the grid system to enlarge the various designs given in Illus. 16-3 to any size to fit your specific location. In general, trellises are not less than 6 feet high. But since there are no specific rules about this, they can be virtually any size. Your own full-size patterns for a 6-foot trellis can be developed from Illus. 16-3. Use a scale of ½ inch equals one foot. Place a ½-inch grid over the design and transfer it square by square to a grid of 6-inch squares. Or, use a ratio of ¼-inch squares to 3-inch squares for re-creating more complicated designs.

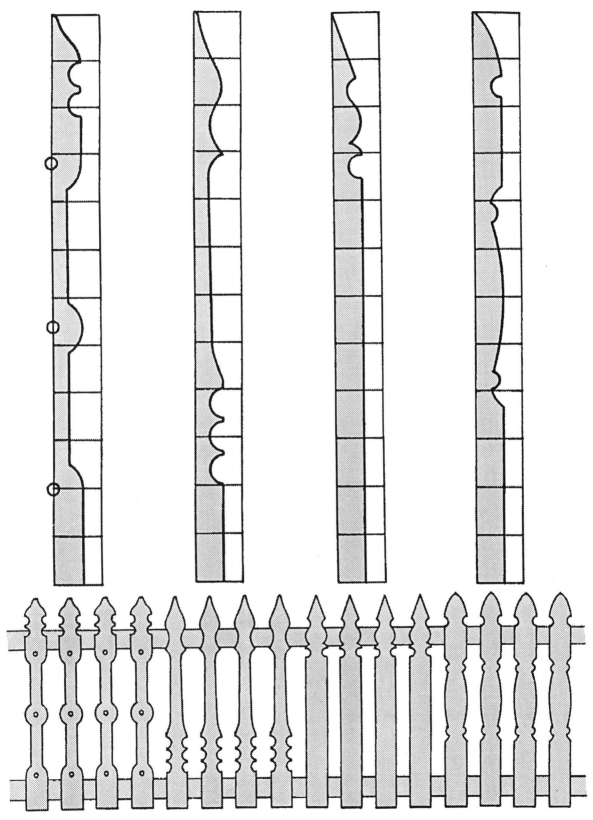

Illus. 16-1. The above are half patterns, to be drawn on 3-inch-square grids.

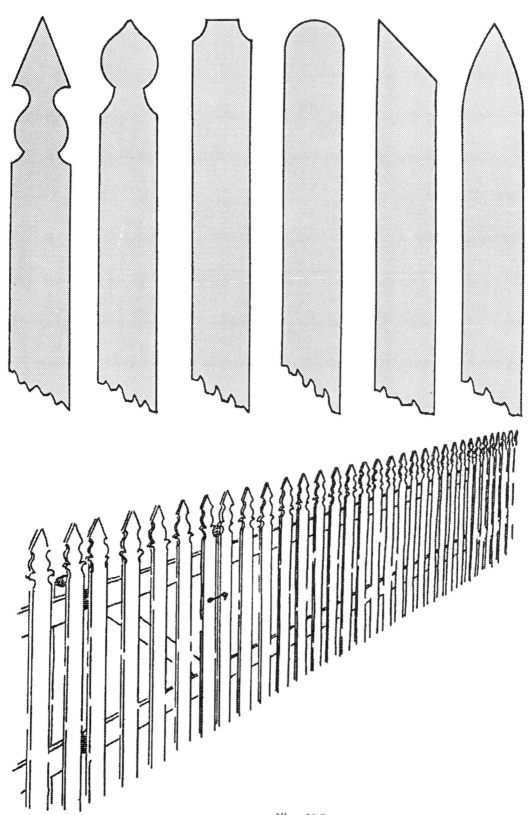

Illus. 16-2.

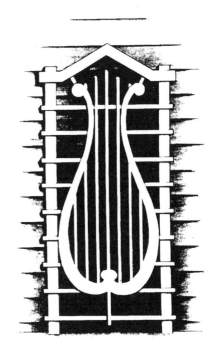

Illus. 16-3.

VICTORIAN MAILBOXES

Probably no other item is more overlooked from the overall architectural scheme of things than the rural mailbox. Anything less than some sort of Victorian motif on your mailbox is a serious oversight (Illus. 17-1). This chapter presents a number of different plans for those who want to unify the overall visual impact of their homes. For city or urban homes, imagine the delight of a rural mailbox set in the ground next to the porch, stoop, or walk. Our mailboxes (Illus. 17-1 and 17-2) make bold Victorian statements. The best part is, they are easy to make and the plans can be modified easily to incorporate even less complicated construction methods if you wish.

Illus. 17-1. An arm-type mailbox post with decorative Victorian brackets and a running-trim design.

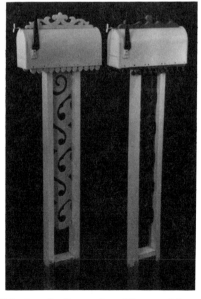

Illus. 17-2. Standard metal mailboxes with ornamental headers and decorative mounting boards that sit on posts of double 2 × 4's with grille construction.

Illus. 17-3. Some header designs selected to decorate the tops of rural metal mailboxes. These are cut from stock ¾ to 1½ inches in thickness.

Illus. 17-4. Bevel rip cuts, with the blade set at 5 to 7 degrees, permit headers or brackets to fit into the curvature of the mailbox shown in Illus. 17-5.

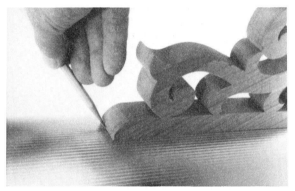

Illus. 17-5. A shallow "V," cut on the bottom of the header, makes a nice fit to the round surface of the box.

Illus. 17-6. Notching around the door catch.

Illus. 17-7. Notch the bracket as shown for a tight fit around the raised rear flange of the mailbox. The back of the mailbox is screwed to the post and the bracket is screwed to the box from the inside.

Illus. 17-8. Examples of decorative mounting boards that fit into the flanged cavity under all metal rural mailboxes. The box is attached to the mounting board with screws driven through the holes in the sides of the box.

Gingerbread ornamentation can be developed around a regular, rural metal mailbox in three ways: (1) Screw a decorative header (Illus. 17-3) on top of the metal box from the inside, using sheet-metal screws. (2) Make a decorative mounting board that sits on the post but is visible from under the box. (3) Add brackets or grille ornamentation to the post. The components shown here are interchangeable, or you can use other patterns and designs from this book or your own sources.

Decorative Headers (Illus. 17-3 to 17-7) ***and Brackets.*** The quickest way to give your mailbox a Victorian feel is with decorative headers and brackets mounted on the top of the box. Simply enlarge the header patterns given on pages 128 and 129 by 125% — or until they are approximately 17 inches long. Illus. 17-4 to 17-7 show some techniques for making a shallow "V" cut along the bottom edge and for making various notches to fit around metal screws and raised flanges.

Decorative Mounting Boards (Illus. 17-8) set off the mailbox nicely. Use them to dress up the tops of posts already set into the ground or with any of the post designs that appear here. All mounting boards have repeating, continuous-trim designs. Many other designs can be adapted from other patterns. Make the pieces from stock ¾ inch in thickness. Most standard no. 1-size metal mailboxes have a 6⅛-inch-wide bottom cavity.

The mounting boards must be shorter than the length of the metal box to allow room for the door, which swings down and also back slightly as it's opened. Most mounting boards are made from three pieces of wood ¾ inch thick. See Illus. 17-9. Two continuous trim pieces are fastened to the edges of a connecting piece that is 4½ inches in width.

Illus. 17-9. A decorative mounting board on an arm-type post. Note how this one is made from three pieces of stock ¾ inches in thickness.

167

Full-size patterns for the side-trim pieces of the mounting boards are given in Illus. 17-10 and 17-14. Another design with balls and dowels dropping from a single-piece mounting board is shown in Illus. 17-12. *Tip:* It may be necessary to slip a 6 × 17½-inch filler board in between the metal box and the mounting board to show the appropriate amount of trim decoration. The cavities under various brands of metal boxes may vary ⅜ to ½ inch in vertical space or depth; this amount may be needed to shim up the mailbox to achieve the best overall look.

Double 2 × 4 Posts (Illus. 17-10, 17-12, and 17-14). This type of construction provides a way to incorporate a fretted or scroll-patterned grille into a post design to carry out the gingerbread theme. It's best to use two carefully selected pressure-treated 2 × 4s that are no less than 68 inches long vertically. The decorative grilles can be cut from ½-inch or ¾-inch plywood or solid wood. Make the grilles so the exposed distance between the insides of the two 2 × 4s is approximately 5½ inches. If you enlarge the given patterns five and one quarter times, this will give you the full-size pattern.

Note on the drawings that each decorative grille is designed with tabs that fit into slotted mortises cut into the vertical 2 × 4s. See Illus. 17-16 to 17-18. This strong form of construction is optional if you have a router. Alternatively, run vertical grooves uninterrupted down the full length on the inside surfaces of each 2 × 4.

Arm-Type Mailbox Post (Illus. 17-1, 17-9, and the drawing, Illus. 17-19). This design makes a beautiful and dramatic statement in front of your Victorian home. The construction is relatively simple and straightforward. The drawing (Illus. 17-19) and the supporting photos show how to make and assemble the post components.

Begin with a 4 × 4 post that is at least 7 feet in overall length. Cut a dado 1¼ inches deep (to receive the arm), 17¼ inches measured from the top of the 4 × 4 post but just under the plate cap. The total length of horizontal arm should be 17¾ inches. Notice that the arm-to-vertical-post assembly shown in Illus. 17-19 and 17-20 utilizes a single lag bolt, ⅜ × 6 inches in length. This bolt anchors into a one-inch-diameter vertical dowel inset near the joint end of the horizontal arm. The other details are described in the captioned photos, Illus. 17-21 and 17-22.

Illus. 17-23 and 17-24 give full-size plans and show an assembled post consisting of one 4 × 4 × 68-inch post with two facing scroll brackets.

Tips: Should you want or need to have street or box numbers on your post, they can be applied vertically to the arm post and to the single post. Use exterior plywood

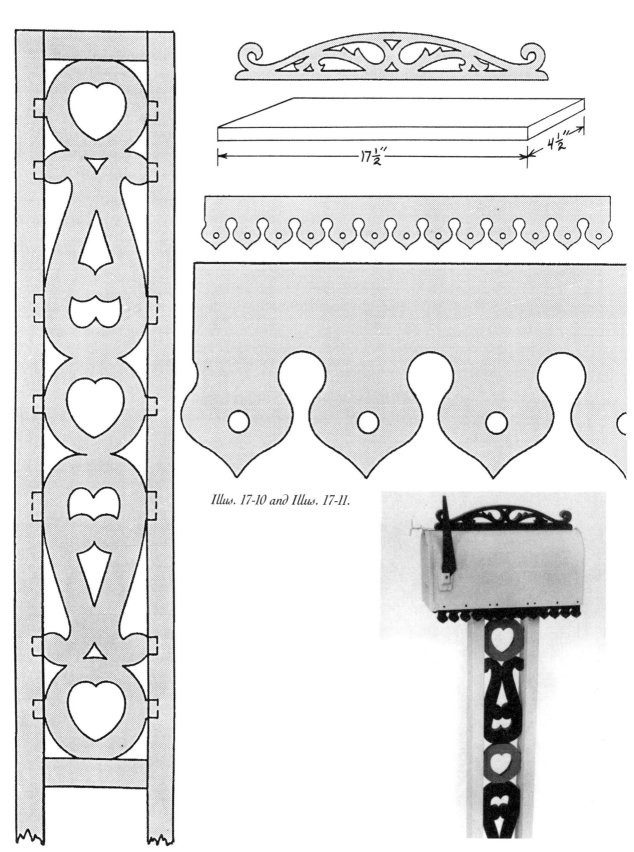

Illus. 17-10 and Illus. 17-11.

17½″ 4½″

169

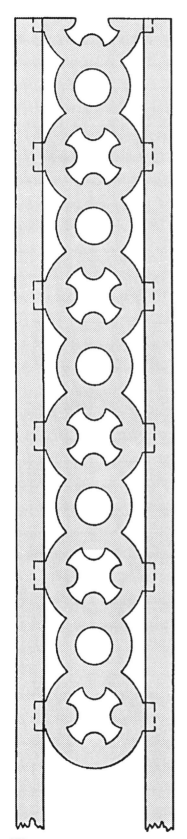

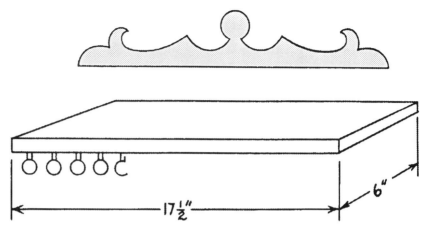

17½"

6"

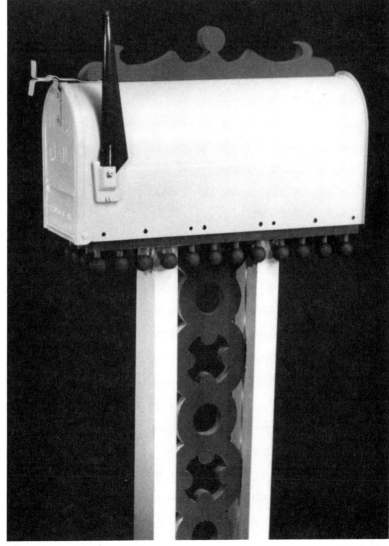

Illus. 17-12 and Illus. 17-13.

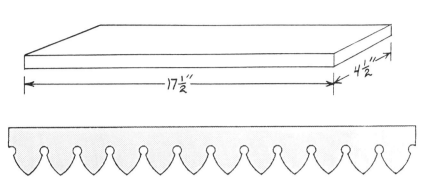

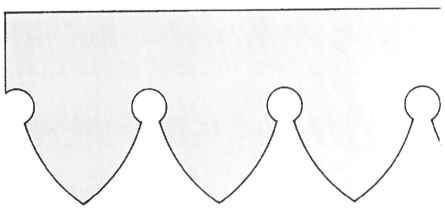

Illus. 17-14 and Illus. 17-15. The mounting board shown here is decorated with 1-inch balls and 3/8-inch dowels. They are spaced 1½ inches on center along the sides. Drill the holes on lines ³/4 inches in from the edges.

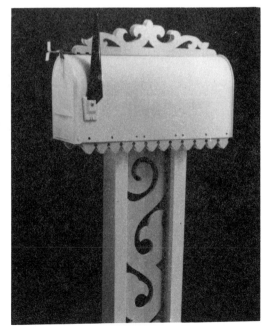

171

Illus. 17-16. Sawing a grille from exterior plywood.

Illus. 17-17. The tabs on the grille fit matching routed-slot mortises cut into pressure-treated 2 × 4's. An alternate method is to simply groove the full length using a router or power circular saw.

Illus. 17-18. Setup for routing the mortise slots in the 2 × 4 posts.

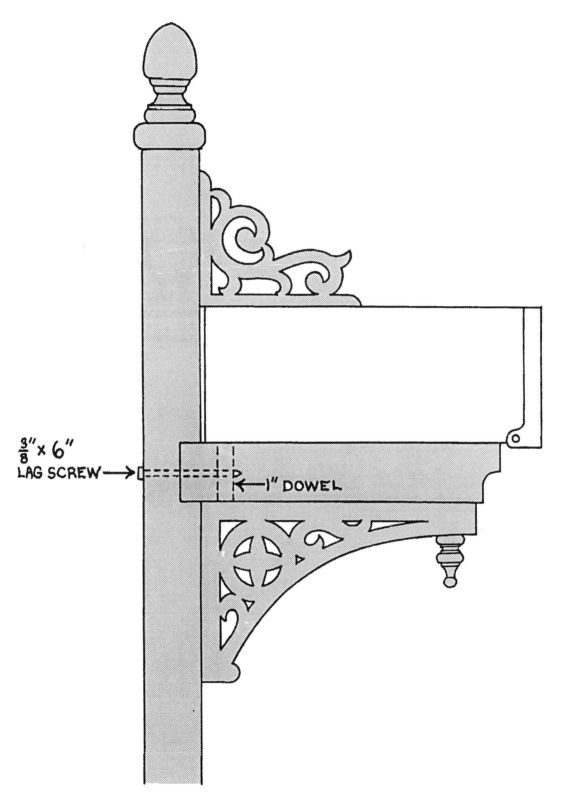

$\frac{3}{8}'' \times 6''$
LAG SCREW →

1" DOWEL

Illus. 17-19. Details of an arm-type mailbox post. The pattern for the upper bracket is shown on page 129. The one for the lower bracket is on page 70.

Illus. 17-20. The essential details of the arm-to-post construction. Note the recessed dado cut into the vertical post and the 1-inch dowel in the arm. The dowel provides exceptional strength to the joint by providing a good anchor for the ⅜ × 6-inch connecting lag bolt.

Illus. 17-22. Mounting a bracket. A 10d finish nail (with the head cut off) is used as a bit to predrill nail holes, to prevent splintering. Using glue is also advisable.

Illus. 17-21. A turned finial sets off the top of the post. Use a purchased finial or turn your own. The plate cap measures 1½ × 4½ inches square.

or solid wood, and saw out the appropriate numbers from the choice of letter and number patterns given in the next chapter. Glue and tack them to the post so they read vertically. Finally, check your local postal regulations before installing your post. Some curbside deliveries prefer the inside bottom of the box to be a specific distance from the street. Rural boxes, when installed along country roads, are usually set 42 inches from the ground to the bottom of the mailbox.

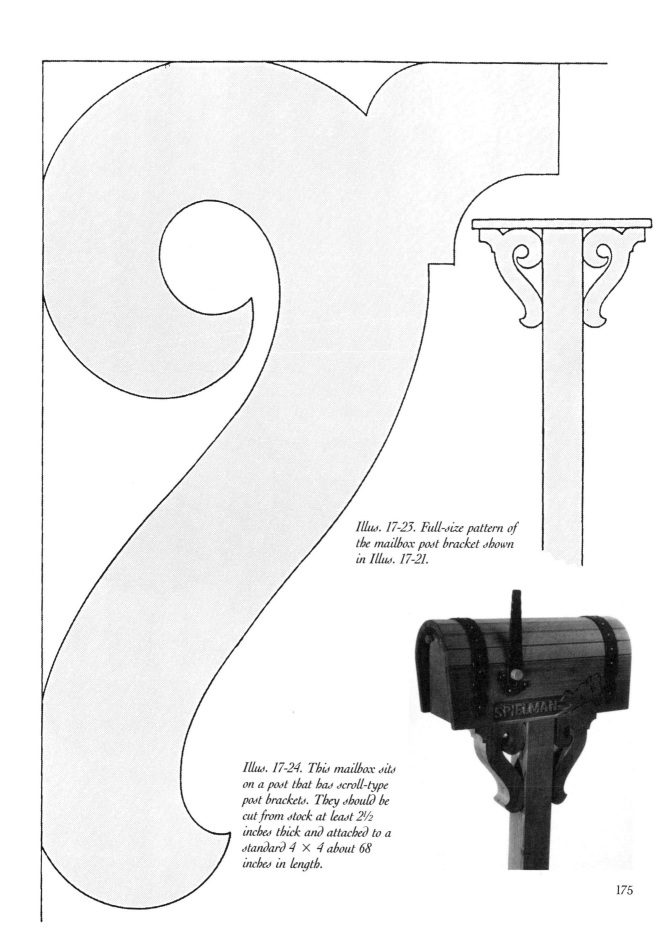

Illus. 17-23. Full-size pattern of the mailbox post bracket shown in Illus. 17-21.

Illus. 17-24. This mailbox sits on a post that has scroll-type post brackets. They should be cut from stock at least 2½ inches thick and attached to a standard 4 × 4 about 68 inches in length.

VICTORIAN SIGNS

A charming sign displaying your house numbers (Illus. 18-1) and/or a sign just to say "Welcome" (Illus. 18-2), or one with the family or estate name is an important final touch to the Victorian home design theme. This chapter presents two pattern designs (Illus. 18-3 and 18-4) for signs that can be hung or mounted against a wall. Also included are patterns for an entire ornate alphabet in an easy-to-read Victorian style. There is even a choice of two different styles of numbers. See Illus. 18-5 and 18-6. We have also included details for making a Victorian signpost for the yard or for a roadside installation. See Illus. 18-15.

The ability to cut sharp curves and to cut outlines of a very small radius can now be achieved easily with the new scroll-cutting band saws and the new constant-tension scroll saws. These enable woodworkers to make beautiful wood signs with ornate letters and distinctive backing boards. Raised wood letters, border scrolls, turnings, and optional carving features can be combined to make some very distinctive and attractive signs in the Victorian style.

The easiest way to make a raised border is to saw it from separate stock and then attach it to the sign-board backer. The thickness of the border stock should be about ¼ inch for the patterns given in Illus. 18-3 and 18-4. If for any reason you enlarge these patterns more than suggested, be sure to make the borders proportionally thicker. If your sign-board backer is cut from plywood, then you can use ¼-inch exterior plywood for border material and also for the numbers or letters. If you use solid wood for the sign board, use solid wood or plywood ¼-inch thick for cutting the letters or numbers and for any border pieces.

Tip: For borders, letters, and numbers that are to be mounted to solid-wood backer boards, be sure to align the grain of *all* pieces and segments so they run in the

Illus. 18-1. House-numbers sign features ¼-inch-thick raised letters and borders.

Illus. 18-2. This welcome or name sign features raised lettering and a border design with decorative turnings and ornate plugs carved from dowels. The mounting fasteners (if used) at each corner are concealed.

Illus. 18-3. Full-size half-pattern signboard suitable for house numbers or other message.

Illus. 18-4. Half-size half pattern for the welcome signboard and the border detail. Note the drill holes for the dowels and the finial locations before sawing out the signboard. Note: Enlarge this pattern 40 percent (140 percent on a photocopier) to make the size of the welcome sign shown in Illus. 18-2.

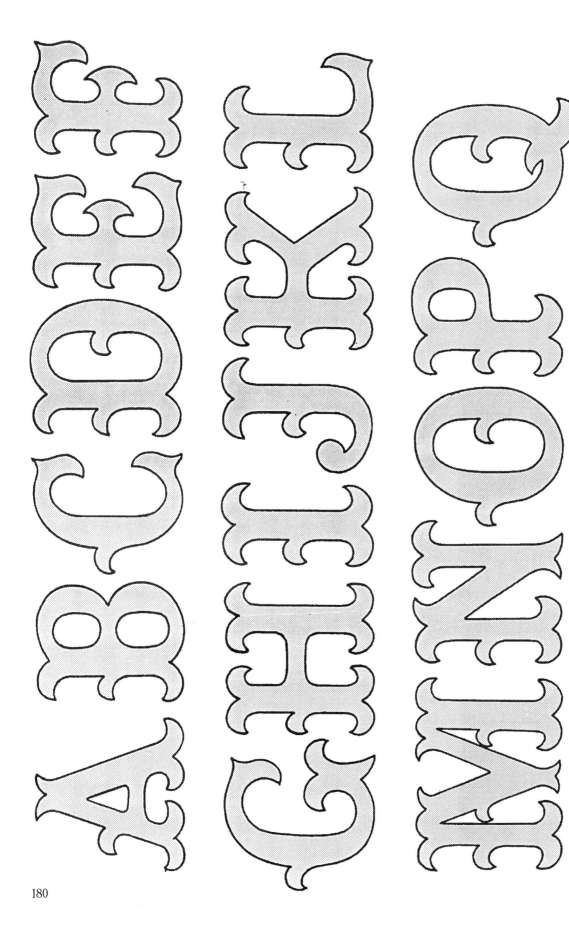

Illus. 18-5 and Illus. 18-6. An ornamental Victorian alphabet with matching number designs. Enlarge the sign-blank pattern in Illus. 18-4 by 40 percent (140 percent on a photocopier).

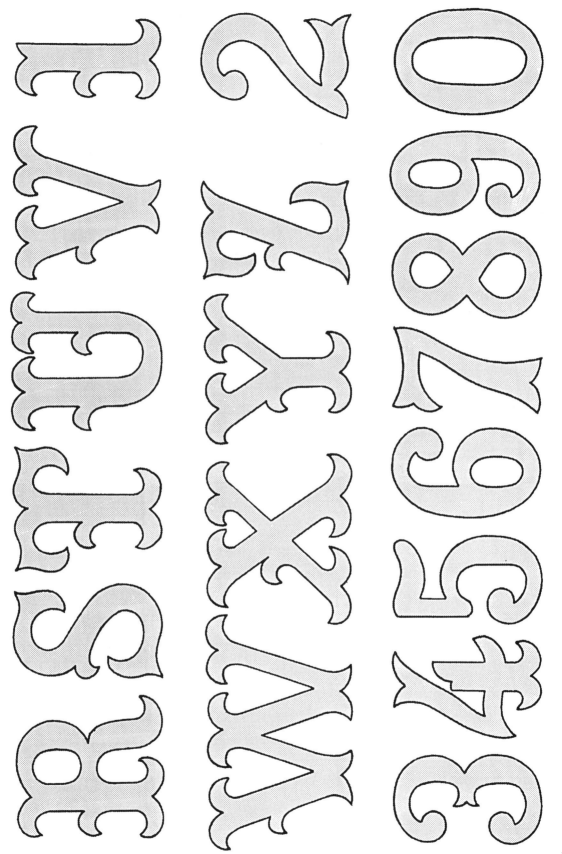

Illus. 18-7. House-number patterns. Enlarge 150 percent to use with the full-size half pattern given in Illus. 18-3.

same direction. Since solid wood expands and shrinks with changes in humidity, each component of the sign will move in harmony, thereby minimizing serious cracking and checking.

There are two ways to cut out the border. You can cut it in segments of two, or four, layers at one time. See Illus. 18-8. Whether or not the sign will be single- or double-faced will determine how many identical pieces you need. The border segments can be butted end-to-end, as necessary. See Illus. 18-9. Actually, stack-sawing is a great advantage, saving time and material. Both halves (or all four quarter-segments) of the border pieces will be identical.

Alternatively, the border piece can be sawn from one thin board presawn to the same size and shape as the backer board. See Illus. 18-10. If you choose this method, cut the outside profile of the sign-board backer and the outside shape of the border stock when the two pieces are stacked together.

Glue and tack the border pieces using waterproof adhesive and short brads (½ inch × no. 20). Tack sparingly, as this is simply to hold the stock tight to the backer board until the glue sets. You can also clamp or tape the border down if you don't want to use nails. See Illus. 18-11 and 18-12.

The welcome-sign pattern calls for four decorative round-corner plugs. They are just short lengths (about ⅝ inch) of ¾-inch-diameter dowel stock with precarved ends. See Illus. 18-13 and 18-14. When wall mounted, these plugs also conceal flat screws. Otherwise they are decorative only.

The Victorian Signpost, as designed in Illus. 18-15, is intended to carry a sign blank 20 inches in width. The arm can be extended or shortened to accommodate other sizes of sign-board patterns.

Illus. 18-8. A technique for making raised borders. Here, two layers of border scrolls are cut at one time by stacking them together.

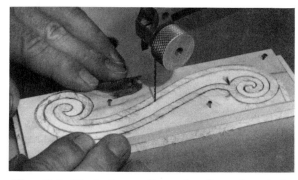

Illus. 18-9. The border scrolls are butted together, glued and tacked to the sign blank. The two vertical pieces are made with "short grain" so they will expand or contract in harmony with any movement of the thicker sign-backer board.

Illus. 18-10. Scroll-sawing a one-piece border from ¼-inch-thick pine.

Illus. 18-11. Small wire brads ½ inch × no. 20 and waterproof glue permanently set the borders.

Illus. 18-12. Letters or numbers are sawn from solid wood, with the grain running in the same direction as the signboard. They are attached with waterproof glue and brads.

Illus. 18-13. An eight-pointed star design is carved into the ends of ¾-inch-diameter dowel stock. Use a "V"-parting tool to make decorative plugs for the four corners of the welcome sign shown in Illus. 18-2.

Illus. 18-14. A completed dowel-end carved design before it is sawn off the end of this dowel stock.

Illus. 18-15. Victorian signpost and sign. Many other bracket designs could also be used. The signboard is created from a simple header design pattern from page 129. The signboard is 20 inches in overall length.

Any number of different hanging sign-board designs can be created using the many header designs given in Chapter 12 to decorate the top or bottom edges. The hanging sign board shown in Illus. 18-15 is a typical example. It was sawn from 1½-inch-thick cedar decking material glued edge to edge.

The post detail is shown in Illus. 18-16 and 18-17. This is essentially the very same construction employed to make the arm-type mailbox post described in the previous chapter. Refer to page 174, which illustrates some of the assembly details.

Normally the vertical post should not be shorter than 8 feet or longer than 10 feet overall. This length is strongly recommended. It allows adequate material for in-ground installation. The horizontal arm is cut to 25½ inches overall to accommodate a sign 20 inches wide. The arm should be dadoed into the vertical post approximately 1¼ inch deep. This cut or recess should begin 12 inches downwards from the top plate. The plate (under the turned finial) is simply a 1½-inch-thick plank cut 4½ inches square with ½-inch-radius rounded edges. Simply nail it onto the end of the post.

Illus. 18-16. Victorian signpost details. The horizontal 4 × 4 arm is 25¼ inches in overall length, including 1¼ inches of it dadoed into the vertical post. This dado cut begins 12 inches from the top-plate cap. A ⅜ × 6-inch lag is anchored into a one-inch dowel, which is inserted vertically near the joint end of the horizontal arm.

The horizontal-arm-to-vertical-post assembly requires a ⅜ × 6-inch lag bolt. It is driven into the end of the 4 × 4-inch arm. However, note on the drawing (Illus. 18-16) and in Illus. 17-20 on page 174 that a 1-inch-diameter dowel is preset vertically into the arm near its attached end. This provides a secure anchor for the lag bolt, making a very strong right-angle joint.

The bracket (Illus. 18-17) is essentially decorative in purpose. It can be from ¾ to 1½ inches in overall thickness and may be glued into place. If it is prepainted, simply tack it on with corrosion-proof finishing nails set below the surface, and fill the holes. There are a number of other flat, sawn bracket-pattern designs from Chapter 4 that can also be sized to fit the bracket area on the signpost.

Finally, numbers can be attached vertically to the signpost, if desired. Simply enlarge the individual patterns (Illus. 18-6 or 18-7) so that each number measures around 3½ inches in height. Cut the numbers from solid wood or plywood. Paint them a contrasting color and attach them with silicon cement, finishing nails, or screws.

Illus. 18-17. The bracket pattern for the Victorian signpost. Enlarge to approximately 20 inches in overall length.

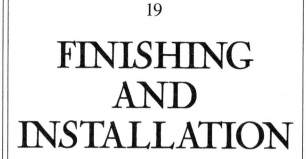

19

FINISHING AND INSTALLATION

After you have cut out the components, you can use the finishing materials and colors of your choice. See Illus. 19-1. Sometimes it will be easier to finish individual parts before making the final assembly. See Illus. 19-2. Generally, finishing involves three areas of work: (1) inside or interior finishing, (2) priming and painting exterior components, and (3) final installation. The best finishing materials are the ones you are most familiar with and comfortable using.

Interior Work can be finished natural (Illus. 9-3) or painted. For natural finishes we recommend penetrating-oil finishes. These are easy to apply with a rag or foam brush. Apply liberally, wipe the excess off the surfaces, and you're done. Staining presents some problems, especially on softwoods, such as pine. It is difficult to get uniform tones, and the results are likely to be blotchy. If you are intent on using a wood-stain finish, test the stain on scrap wood first.

Illus. 19-1. Some basic finishing materials for outside applications include water-repellant preservatives and Latex (or oil-based) enamels.

Illus. 19-2. Where possible, finish parts before assembly. Here the two sides of a corbel are painted a different color before being fastened to the core with finishing nails.

Illus. 19-3. Ornate brackets and other Victorian fret-work are easily finished using penetrating oils liberally applied with rags or a foam brush.

Illus. 19-4. Foam brushes are great for applying latex or water-based enamels.

For painted finishes, be sure to coordinate your colors with your overall design scheme. Almost all pigmented paints will work, because weathering and moisture penetration are not a problem with interior work. Acrylics and flat latex paints are recommended because they cover well and they dry quickly. See Illus. 19-4.

Painting Lathe (Illus. 19-5 to 19-8). For painting multicolored spindles and finials, a painting lathe is an enormous time saver. Use it for applying paints to inside or outside work. This device is very easy to make. It incorporates a variable-speed hand drill as its power supply and speed control. You will need a variable-speed-type hand drill that starts at 0 rpm and can be slowly accelerated to the optimum speed for the work being spun for painting.

Note that the painting lathe unit is designed to be clamped to a bench with it partly extended over the forward edge of the bench. A properly located dowel extending downwards through a hole in the baseboard becomes the switch and speed control. The speed-control dowel lever is operated by applying knee pressure. See Illus. 19-5. This causes the dowel in the baseboard to pivot, thereby triggering the drill switch.

Exterior Painting. It is always best to pretreat outside woodwork with a preservative. Use a good moisture repellant. Apply it very liberally to all areas, but especially well to all end-grain surfaces. You may even want to soak your wood in a vat or shallow tray for 5 to 15 minutes. Allow the wood to dry at least 24 hours before applying any type of sealer-primer.

Always prime your wood before applying a top coat of paint to it. It may be necessary to seal out natural blemishes or other marks that tend to bleed through top-

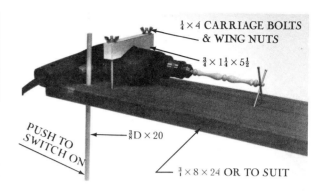

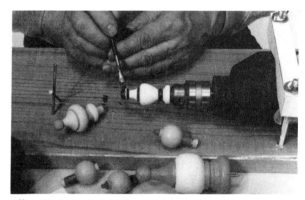

Illus. 19-6. Basic details for making a simple leg-controlled painting lathe using a ³⁄₈-inch variable-speed drill for power. This is designed to extend slightly over the edge of a table or bench, as shown in Illus. 19-5.

Illus. 19-5. Painting spindles, balls, and other turnings before assembly is faster and much easier than after assembly. Here a homemade painting lathe makes quick work of painting multicolored spindles. The operator starts and controls the speed with his knee by applying pressure against the dowel, as shown.

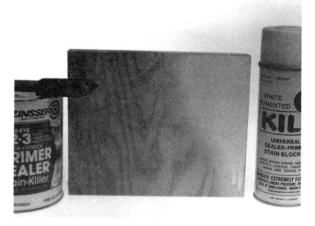

Illus. 19-7. A close look at painting multicolored finials on the turning lathe, which spins the work slowly against your loaded brush.

Illus. 19-8. Painting spindles is done just as easily. The "tail stock" end is simply two crossed nails supporting the free end of the spindle.

Illus. 19-9. Special sealers are available to hide such natural blemishes in wood as knots and the wild grain of fir plywood.

coat finishes. Special sealer-primers (Illus. 19-9) are available that permanently hide knots, the wild grain patterns of fir plywood.

Consider your exterior color combinations very carefully. Properly coordinating color combinations is an art that should be cultivated. Consult with an expert decorator, if necessary. The contemporary trend is towards fairly brash color combinations. These are preferable to all-white arrangements.

Major paint companies sell historical colors, so you can match turn-of-the-century colors. Good paint manufacturers offer custom colorizing with excellent color retention and mildew resistance. However, even the best paints can peel and fail if moisture gets into wood.

Installation Tips. Some experts recommend installing exterior brackets and the like in a bed of caulking. This not only acts as an adhesive, but it helps keep moisture away from the end grains, which are most susceptible to decay and paint failure. Lay a small bead of caulking along any cracks or openings that could absorb water.

To prevent your wood from splitting, always be sure to predrill it for metal fasteners. Use good, corrosion-resistant metal fasteners for all outside installations. Aluminum or galvanized nails and screws are strongly recommended. Be sure to set the heads below the surfaces, and then fill the surfaces over with wood putty or solid wood plugs glued into counter-bored holes.

Metric Equivalents

MM — MILLIMETRES   CM — CENTIMETRES

INCHES TO MILLIMETRES AND CENTIMETRES

INCHES	MM	CM		INCHES	CM		INCHES	CM
1/8	3	0.3		9	22.9		30	76.2
1/4	6	0.6		10	25.4		31	78.7
3/8	10	1.0		11	27.9		32	81.3
1/2	13	1.3		12	30.5		33	83.8
5/8	16	1.6		13	33.0		34	86.4
3/4	19	1.9		14	35.6		35	88.9
7/8	22	2.2		15	38.1		36	91.4
1	25	2.5		16	40.6		37	94.0
1 1/4	32	3.2		17	43.2		38	96.5
1 1/2	38	3.8		18	45.7		39	99.1
1 3/4	44	4.4		19	48.3		40	101.6
2	51	5.1		20	50.8		41	104.1
2 1/2	64	6.4		21	53.3		42	106.7
3	76	7.6		22	55.9		43	109.2
3 1/2	89	8.9		23	58.4		44	111.8
4	102	10.2		24	61.0		45	114.3
4 1/2	114	11.4		25	63.5		46	116.8
5	127	12.7		26	66.0		47	119.4
6	152	15.2		27	68.6		48	121.9
7	178	17.8		28	71.1		49	124.5
8	203	20.3		29	73.7		50	127.0

About the Authors

Patrick Spielman's love of wood began when, as a child, he transformed fruit crates into toys. Now this prolific and innovative woodworker is respected worldwide as a teacher and author.

His most famous contribution to the woodworking field has been his perfection of a method to season green wood with polyethylene glycol 1000 (PEG). He went on to invent, manufacture and distribute the PEG-Thermovat chemical seasoning system.

During his many years as shop instructor in Wisconsin, Spielman published manuals, teaching guides and more than 24 popular books, including *Modern Wood Technology*, a college text. He also wrote six educational series on wood technology, tool use, processing techniques, design and wood-product planning.

Author of the best-selling *Router Handbook*, Spielman has served as editorial consultant to a professional magazine as an adviser and consultant to power tool manufacturers, and his products, techniques and many books have been featured in numerous periodicals.

This pioneer of new ideas and inventor of countless jigs, fixtures and designs used throughout the world is a unique combination of expert woodworker and brilliant teacher — all of which have endeared him to his many readers and to his publisher.

At Spielmans Wood Works in the woods of northern Door County, Wisconsin, he and his family create and sell some of the most durable and popular furniture products and designs available.

Co-author James Reidle has been doing fancy woodwork along with general carpentry all his life. He grew up watching his father create magnificent pieces of scroll-saw fretwork on treadle-type scroll saws. Years later, he wanted to recapture the best features of the early scroll saws his father used, so he developed one of his own, which is especially designed for fretwork and fine-detail scroll sawing. In addition, Reidle developed the first mail-order business in a number of years that is mainly devoted to fretwork patterns and supplies.

INDEX

Arm-type mailbox posts, 168, 173–174
Assembly techniques, 29, 99
Ball-and-dowel spandrels, 9, 111
Balls, 14, 15
Balusters, 116–121
Band saws, 24–25
Beads, 14, 15
Boring, 21–23
Brackets, 114
  frame edges, 30
  installation, 31
  for mailboxes, 165–166, 167, 174, 175
  patterns, 33–76
  for screen doors, 160
  for signpost, 185–186
  uses, 31–32
Coping saw, 21
Copy machine enlargements, 16
Corbels, 30
  making, 77, 79
  patterns, 78–90
  uses, 77
Designs, 8–9
Disc sander, 27
Doorway headers, 127–137
Double 2 × 4 mailbox posts, 168–170
Drilling, 21–23
Duraply, 14
Enlargement of patterns, 16–18, 161
Exterior painting, 188–190
Fan brackets, 9, 30
  assembly, 99
  ball-and-dowel, 94, 96, 100–102
  drilling guide, 97–98
  layout board, 94, 97
  making, 94, 97–99
  patterns, 96, 100–103
  for screen doors, 160
  spindle type, 94, 95, 103
  types, 94
Finials, 14–15
Finishing
  exterior painting, 188–190
  interior work, 187–188

Gable ornaments, 7
  finding angle for trim, 147–148
  modifying, 147–148
  patterns, 149–157
Glues, 13, 29
Grain direction, 19
Grid system, 16–18, 161
Grilles, 104, 106, 172
  layout, 107
  making, 107
Hardware, shelf-mounting, 91–92
Headers
  for doorway, 127–137
  for mailboxes, 166, 167
Installation tips, 190
Interior arch grille colonnade, 6
Interior openings, 7
Jig saws, 25
Lathe, painting, 188
Layout
  for grilles and spandrels, 107
  of patterns, 16–20
Layout board, for fan brackets, 94, 97
Letters, Victorian, 180–181
Mahogany, 12
Mailbox ornamentation, 10, 129, 165–175
Mailbox posts
  arm-type, 168, 173–174
  double 2 × 4, 168–170
Mouldings, 14
Mounting boards, for mailboxes, 166,
  167, 171
Numbers, Victorian, 181–182
Oak, 12–13
Painting lathe, 188
Panel materials, 13
Patterns
  for brackets, 33–76
  for corbels, 78–90
  enlargement, 16–19
  for fan brackets, 96, 100–103
  for gable ornaments, 149–157
  layout, 16–20
  for signboard, 178–179

  transferring, 18–19
Penetrating-oil finishes, 187
Picket fences, 161–163
Pine, 12–13
Pivoting block, 98
Plywood, 13–14
Porch spandrels, 108–115
Redwood, 12
Roof pitch, 147–148
Routing, 27–29
Running trim, 122–126
Safety, 21
Sanding, 26–27
Sawing, 24–26
Sawn brackets, 7–8, 30–76
Screen doors, 158–160
Scroll saws, 25
Shaping, 27–29
Shelf hangers, 91–93
Signboard pattern, 178–179
Signposts, 183–186
Signs, 176–186
  lettering for, 180–181
  making, 176, 183
  numbering for, 181–182
  signboard pattern, 178–179
Smoothing, 26–27
Softwoods, 11–12
Spandrels, 104–105
  layout, 107
  making, 107
  porch, 108–115
Templates, 19
Tool processes, 21–29. *See also specific
  tools and/or processes*
Transferring of pattern, 18–19
Trellises, 161, 164
Trim, running, 122–126
"Turning-hole" strategy, 20, 24
Turnings, 14
Valances, 138–146
Victorian letters, 180–181
Victorian numbers, 181–182
Wood, solid, 11–12